# MONEY, ECONOMICS, AND FINANCE

# DEVELOPMENTS, ANALYSES AND RESEARCH

# VOLUME 3

# MONEY, ECONOMICS, AND FINANCE: DEVELOPMENTS, ANALYSES AND RESEARCH

MONEY, ECONOMICS, AND FINANCE:
DEVELOPMENTS, ANALYSES AND RESEARCH

# MONEY, ECONOMICS, AND FINANCE

## DEVELOPMENTS, ANALYSES AND RESEARCH

## VOLUME 3

### CLIFFORD DOBROWSKI
### EDITOR

publishers

*New York*

**Library of Congress Cataloging-in-Publication Data**

ISSN: 2325-9426

ISBN: 978-1-63321-505-4

*Published by Nova Science Publishers, Inc.* † *New York*

# CONTENTS

# PREFACE

In this third book of the series "Money, Economics, and Finance: Developments, Analyses, and Research", topics discussed include bitcoin; current debates over exchange rates; recent trends in consumer retail payment services delivered by depository institutions; financial condition of depository banks; government assistance for AIG; and investment advisers.

Chapter 1 - Bitcoin first appeared in January 2009, the creation of a computer programmer using the pseudonym Satoshi Nakamoto. His invention is an open source (its controlling computer code is open to public view), peer to peer (transactions do not require a third-party intermediary such as PayPal or Visa), digital currency (being electronic with no physical manifestation). The Bitcoin system is private, but with no traditional financial institutions involved in transactions. Unlike earlier digital currencies that had some central controlling person or entity, the Bitcoin network is *completely decentralized*, with all parts of transactions performed by the users of the system.

With a Bitcoin transaction there is no third party intermediary. The buyer and seller interact directly (peer to peer) but their identities are encrypted and no personal information is transferred from one to the other. However, unlike a fully anonymous transaction, there is a transaction record. A full transaction record of every Bitcoin and every Bitcoin user's encrypted identity is maintained on the public ledger. For this reason Bitcoin transactions are thought to be pseudonymous, not anonymous. Although the scale of Bitcoin use has increased substantially, it still remains small in comparison to traditional electronic payments systems such as credit cards and the use of dollars as a circulating currency.

Congress is interested in Bitcoin because of concerns about its use in illegal money transfers, concerns about its effect on the ability of the Federal

Reserve to meet its objectives (of stable prices, maximum employment, and financial stability), and concerns about the protection of consumers and investors who might use it.

Bitcoin offers users the advantages of lower transaction costs, increased privacy, and long term protection of loss of purchasing power from inflation. However, there are also a number of disadvantages that could hinder wider use. These include sizable volatility of the price of Bitcoins, uncertain security from theft and fraud, and a long term deflationary bias that encourages the hoarding of Bitcoins.

Bitcoin also raises a number of legal and regulatory concerns including its potential for facilitating money laundering, its treatment under federal securities law, and its status in the regulation of foreign exchange trading.

Chapter 2 - Exchange rates are important in the international economy, because they affect the price of every country's imports and exports, as well as the value of every overseas investment. Following the global financial crisis of 2008-2009 and ensuing economic recession, disagreements among countries over exchange rates have become more widespread. Some policy leaders and analysts contend that there is a "currency war" now underway among certain countries.

At the heart of current disagreements is whether or not countries are using exchange rate policies to undermine free markets and intentionally push down the value of their currency in order to gain a trade advantage at the expense of other countries. A weak currency makes exports cheaper to foreigners, which can lead to higher exports and job creation in the export sector. However, if one country weakens its currency, there can be implications for other countries. In general, exporters and firms producing import-sensitive goods may find it harder to compete against countries with weak currencies. However, consumers and businesses that rely on inputs from abroad may benefit when other countries have weak currencies, because imports may become cheaper.

The United States has found itself on both sides of the current debates over exchange rates. On one hand, some Members of Congress and U.S. policy experts argue that U.S. exports and U.S. jobs have been adversely affected by the exchange rate policies adopted by China, Japan, and a number of other countries. On the other hand, some emerging markets, including Brazil and Russia, have argued that expansionary monetary policies in the United States and other developed countries caused the currencies of developed countries to depreciate, hurting the competitiveness of emerging markets. More recently, however, emerging-market currencies have started to depreciate, and now there are concerns about emerging-market currencies becoming too weak relative to the currencies of some developed economies.

Through the International Monetary Fund (IMF), countries have committed to avoid "currency manipulation." There are also provisions in U.S. law to address "currency manipulation" by other countries. In the context of recent disagreements, neither the IMF nor the U.S. Treasury Department has determined any country to be manipulating its exchange rate. There are differing views on why. Some argue that countries have not engaged in policies that violate international commitments on exchange rates or triggered provisions in U.S. law relating to currency manipulation. Others argue that currency manipulation has occurred, but that estimating a currency's "true" or "fundamental" value is complicated, and that the current international financial architecture is not effective at responding to exchange rate disputes.

Chapter 3 - Congressional interest in the performance of the credit and debit card (checking account services) markets and how recent developments are affecting customers is growing. This report discusses these developments and examines the costs and availability of consumer retail payments services, particularly those provided by depository institutions, since the recent recession and subsequent legislative actions.

Consumer retail payment services include products such as credit cards, cash advances, checking accounts, debit cards, and prepayment cards. Some depository institutions have increased fees and decreased availability of these services; many others are considering the best way to cover rising costs to provide these services without alienating customers. Recent declines in the demand for loans, a historically and persistently low interest rate environment, higher capital requirements, and the existence of potential profit opportunities in non-traditional banking markets may have motivated these reactions. In addition, passage of the Credit Card Accountability Responsibility and Disclosure Act of 2009 (CARD Act; P.L. 111-24) and Section 920 of the Dodd-Frank Wall Street Reform and Consumer Protection Act of 2010 (Dodd-Frank Act; P.L. 111-203), which is known as the Durbin Amendment, placed limitations on fee income for credit cards and debit cards, respectively.

Determining the extent to which one or all of these factors have influenced changes in the consumer retail payment services markets, however, is challenging. Market outcomes are often influenced by multiple simultaneous or overlapping events, thus making it difficult to attribute the reactions of financial service providers and their customers solely to any one particular factor. Any one or all of the factors listed above that occurred after 2007 may have driven changes in the costs or availability of consumer retail payment services, making it difficult to determine which one had the greatest influence on market outcomes.

Depository institutions reduced credit card loan limits during the recent recession, but those limits have since been rising. Customers with impaired credit, however, have seen increases in credit card rates and reduced access to this product. Many large depository institutions have also discontinued debit card rewards programs and "free" checking. Many small financial institutions have not increased checking account fees as aggressively, but many have increased fees on less frequently used financial services and are considering further fee increases to cover anticipated higher costs. The consumer retail payment services market may also be growing more bifurcated. For example, customers more likely to repay obligations or maintain high checking account balances may experience few changes in costs or availability of traditional payments services. At the same time, customers likely to face higher costs to use or limited access to traditional payment services may increase their usage of direct deposit cash advances and prepayment cards, as depository institutions make these options increasingly available to this market segment.

Chapter 4 - A bank is an institution that obtains either a federal or state charter that allows it to accept federally insured deposits and pay interest to depositors. In addition, the charter allows banks to make residential and commercial mortgage loans; provide check cashing and clearing services; underwrite securities that include U.S. Treasuries, municipal bonds, commercial paper, and Fannie Mae and Freddie Mac issuances; and other activities as defined by statute.

Congressional interest in the financial conditions of depository banks or the commercial banking industry has increased in the wake of the financial crisis that unfolded in 2007-2009, which resulted in a large increase in the number of distressed institutions. A financially strained banking system would have difficulty making credit available to facilitate macroeconomic recovery.

The financial condition of the banking industry can be examined in terms of profitability, lending activity, and capitalization levels (to buffer against the financial risks). This report focuses primarily on profitability and lending activity levels.

The banking industry continues consolidating, with more total assets held by a smaller total number of institutions. There are fewer problem banks since the peak in 2011, as well as fewer bank failures in 2013 in comparison to the peak amount of failures in 2010. Non-current loans still exceed the capacity of the banking industry to absorb potential losses (should they become uncollectible), meaning that news of industry profitability should be tempered by the news that aggregate loan loss provisions are currently insufficient. Consequently, the rate of bank lending growth may not return to pre-crisis levels until loan-loss capacity exhibits even more improvement.

Chapter 5 - American International Group (AIG), one of the world's major insurers, was the largest direct recipient of government financial assistance during the recent financial crisis. At the maximum, the Federal Reserve (Fed) and the Treasury committed approximately $182.3 billion in specific extraordinary assistance for AIG and another $15.9 billion through a more widely available lending facility. The amount actually disbursed to assist AIG reached a maximum of $184.6 billion in April 2009. In return, AIG paid interest and dividends on the funding and the U.S. Treasury ultimately received a 92% ownership share in the company. As of December 14, 2012, the government assistance for AIG ended. All Federal Reserve loans have been repaid and the Treasury has sold all of the common equity that resulted from the assistance.

Going into the financial crisis, the overarching AIG holding company was regulated by the Office of Thrift Supervision (OTS), but most of its U.S. operating subsidiaries were regulated by various states. Because AIG was primarily an insurer, it was largely outside of the normal Federal Reserve facilities that lend to thrifts facing liquidity difficulties and it was also outside of the normal Federal Deposit Insurance Corporation (FDIC) receivership provisions that apply to banking institutions. September 2008 saw a panic in financial markets marked by the failure of large financial institutions, such as Fannie Mae, Freddie Mac, and Lehman Brothers. In addition to suffering from the general market downturn, AIG faced extraordinary losses resulting largely from two sources: (1) the AIG Financial Products subsidiary, which specialized in financial derivatives and was primarily the regulatory responsibility of the OTS; and (2) a securities lending program, which used securities originating in the state-regulated insurance subsidiaries. In the panic conditions prevailing at the time, the Federal Reserve determined that "a disorderly failure of AIG could add to already significant levels of financial market fragility" and stepped in to support the company. Had AIG not been given assistance by the government, bankruptcy seemed a near certainty. The Federal Reserve support was later supplemented and ultimately replaced by assistance from the U.S. Treasury's Troubled Asset Relief Program (TARP).

The AIG rescue produced unexpected financial returns for the government. The Fed loans were completely repaid and it directly received $18.1 billion in interest, dividends, and capital gains. In addition, another

$17.5 billion in capital gains from the Fed assistance accrued to the Treasury. The $67.8 billion in TARP assistance, however, resulted in a negative return to the government, as only $54.4 billion was recouped from asset sales and $0.9 billion was received in dividend payments. If one offsets the negative return to TARP of $12.5 billion with the $35.6 billion in positive returns for the Fed assistance, the entire assistance for AIG showed a positive return of approximately $23.1 billion. It should be noted that these figures are the simple cash returns from the AIG transactions and do not take into account the full economic costs of the assistance. Fully accounting for these costs would result in lower returns to the government, although no agency has performed such a full assessment of the AIG assistance. The latest Congressional Budget Office (CBO) estimate of the budgetary cost of the TARP assistance for AIG, which is a broader economic analysis of the cost, found a loss of $15 billion compared with the $12.5 billion cash loss. CBO does not, however, regularly perform cost estimates on Federal Reserve actions.

Congressional interest in the AIG intervention relates to oversight of the Federal Reserve and TARP, as well as general policy measures to promote financial stability. Specific attention has focused on perceived corporate profligacy, particularly compensation for AIG employees, which was the subject of a hearing in the 113th Congress and legislation in the 111th Congress.

Chapter 6 - Investment advisers provide a wide range of services and collectively manage around $54 trillion in assets for around 24 million clients. Unlike banks and broker-dealers, investment advisers typically do not maintain physical custody of client assets. However, under federal securities regulations, advisers may be deemed to have custody because of their authority to access client assets, for example, by deducting advisory fees from a client account. High-profile fraud cases in recent years highlighted the risks faced by investors when an adviser has custody of their assets. In response, SEC amended its custody rule in 2009 to require a broader range of advisers to undergo annual surprise examinations by independent accountants. At the same time, SEC provided relief from this requirement to certain advisers, including those deemed to have custody solely because of their use of related but "operationally independent" custodians. The Dodd-Frank Wall Street Reform and Consumer Protection Act mandates GAO to study the costs associated with the custody rule. This report describes (1) the requirements of and costs associated with the custody rule and (2) SEC's rationale for not requiring advisers using related but operationally independent custodians to undergo surprise examinations.

To address the objectives, GAO reviewed federal securities laws and related rules, analyzed data on advisers, and met with SEC, advisers, accounting firms, and industry and other associations.

In: Money, Economics, and Finance. Volume 3    ISBN: 978-1-63321-505-4
Editor: Clifford Dobrowski                © 2014 Nova Science Publishers, Inc.

*Chapter 1*

# BITCOIN: QUESTIONS, ANSWERS, AND ANALYSIS OF LEGAL ISSUES[*]

*Craig K. Elwell,*
*M. Maureen Murphy*
*and Michael V. Seitzinger*

## SUMMARY

Bitcoin first appeared in January 2009, the creation of a computer programmer using the pseudonym Satoshi Nakamoto. His invention is an open source (its controlling computer code is open to public view), peer to peer (transactions do not require a third-party intermediary such as PayPal or Visa), digital currency (being electronic with no physical manifestation). The Bitcoin system is private, but with no traditional financial institutions involved in transactions. Unlike earlier digital currencies that had some central controlling person or entity, the Bitcoin network is *completely decentralized*, with all parts of transactions performed by the users of the system.

With a Bitcoin transaction there is no third party intermediary. The buyer and seller interact directly (peer to peer) but their identities are

---

[*] This is an edited, reformatted and augmented version of a Congressional Research Service publication R43339, prepared for Members and Committees of Congress, dated December 20, 2013.

encrypted and no personal information is transferred from one to the other. However, unlike a fully anonymous transaction, there is a transaction record. A full transaction record of every Bitcoin and every Bitcoin user's encrypted identity is maintained on the public ledger. For this reason Bitcoin transactions are thought to be pseudonymous, not anonymous. Although the scale of Bitcoin use has increased substantially, it still remains small in comparison to traditional electronic payments systems such as credit cards and the use of dollars as a circulating currency.

Congress is interested in Bitcoin because of concerns about its use in illegal money transfers, concerns about its effect on the ability of the Federal Reserve to meet its objectives (of stable prices, maximum employment, and financial stability), and concerns about the protection of consumers and investors who might use it.

Bitcoin offers users the advantages of lower transaction costs, increased privacy, and long term protection of loss of purchasing power from inflation. However, there are also a number of disadvantages that could hinder wider use. These include sizable volatility of the price of Bitcoins, uncertain security from theft and fraud, and a long term deflationary bias that encourages the hoarding of Bitcoins.

Bitcoin also raises a number of legal and regulatory concerns including its potential for facilitating money laundering, its treatment under federal securities law, and its status in the regulation of foreign exchange trading.

The digital currency called Bitcoin has been in existence since 2009 and for most of that time it remained little more than a technological curiosity of interest to a small segment of the population. However, over the last year and a half, Bitcoin use has grown substantially; attention by the press has surged, and recently Bitcoin caught the attention of Congress, being the subject of two Senate hearings.[1]

This report has three major sections. The first section answers some basic questions about Bitcoin and the operation of the Bitcoin network and its interaction with the current dollar-based monetary system. The second section summarizes likely reasons for and against widespread Bitcoin adoption. The third section discusses legal and regulatory matters that have been raised by Bitcoin and other digital currencies.

# SOME BASIC QUESTIONS

## What Is Bitcoin? [1]

Bitcoin first appeared in January 2009, the creation of a computer programmer using the pseudonym Satoshi Nakamoto. His invention is an open source (its controlling computer code is open to public view), peer to peer (transactions do not require a third-party intermediary such as PayPal or Visa), digital currency (being electronic with no physical manifestation).[2]

Like the U.S. dollar, the Bitcoin is a *fiat currency* in that it is not redeemable for some amount of another commodity, such as an ounce of gold. Unlike the dollar, a Bitcoin is not legal tender nor is it backed by any government or any other legal entity, nor is its supply determined by a central bank. The Bitcoin system is private, but with no traditional financial institutions involved in transactions. Unlike earlier digital currencies that had some central controlling person or entity, the Bitcoin network is *completely decentralized*, with all parts of transactions performed by the users of the system.

## How Does the Bitcoin System Work?

Bitcoin is sometimes referred to as a cryptocurrency because it relies on the principles of cryptography (communication that is secure from view of third parties) to validate transactions and govern the production of the currency itself. Each Bitcoin and each user is encrypted with a unique identity and each transaction is recorded on a decentralized public ledger (also called a blockchain) that is visible to all computers on the network, but does not reveal any personal information about the involved parties. The public ledger verifies that the buyer has the amount of Bitcoin being spent and has transferred that amount to the account of the seller.

The public ledger is a unique attribute of Bitcoin (and other cryptocurrencies) because it solves the so called *double spending* problem (i.e., spending money you do not own by use of forgery or counterfeiting) and the need for a trusted third party (such as a bank or credit card company) to verify the integrity of electronic transactions between a buyer and a seller.

## How Are Bitcoins Obtained?

To interact on the Bitcoin network users first need to download the free and open-source software. Once connected to the network, there are three ways to obtain Bitcoins. First, a user can exchange conventional money (e.g., dollars, yen, and euros) for a fee on an online exchange (e.g., Mt. Gox, Coinbase, and Kraken). The exchange fee falls with the size of the transaction, ranging from 0.5% for small transactions down to 0.2% for large transactions.

The price of Bitcoin relative to other currencies is determined by supply and demand. In mid-December, 2013, a single Bitcoin was valued at around $800. However, the price has been quite volatile, having been above $1200 in early December and around $200 in early November.[3]

Second, a user can obtain Bitcoins in exchange for the sale of goods or services, as when a merchant accepts Bitcoin from a buyer for the sale of his product.

Third, a user can generate Bitcoins through a process called *mining*. Mining involves applying the user's computer's processing power to solve a complex math problem to discover new Bitcoins. The probability of an individual discovering Bitcoins through mining is proportional to the amount of computer processing power that can be applied. This prospect is likely to be very small for the typical office or home computer. The difficulty of the math problem is such that Bitcoins will be discovered at a limited and predictable rate system wide.

Therefore, the supply of Bitcoins does not depend on the monetary policy of a virtual central bank. In this regard, although a fiat currency, the Bitcoin system's operation is similar to the growth of money under a gold standard, although historically the amount of gold mined was more erratic than the growth of the supply of Bitcoins is purported to be. Depending on one's perspective this attribute can be a virtue or a vice.

Currently, about 12 million Bitcoins are in circulation. However, the total number of Bitcoins that can be generated is arbitrarily capped at 21 million coins, which is predicted to be reached in 2140. Also, because a Bitcoin is divisible to *eight* decimal places, the maximum amount of spendable units is more than *2 quadrillion* (i.e., 2000 trillion).

Purchased or mined Bitcoins are thereafter stored in a digital wallet on the user's computer or at an online wallet service.

## Are Bitcoin Transactions Anonymous?

Bitcoin transactions are not truly anonymous.[4] An example of an anonymous transaction is an exchange for cash between two strangers. In this case, no personal information need be revealed nor does there need to be a record of the transaction. At the other extreme a non-anonymous transaction is a typical online purchase using a credit card. This transaction requires validation by a third-party intermediary to whom the buyer's and seller's identities and pertinent financial information is known and who maintains a record of the transaction. A Bitcoin transaction falls between these two extremes.

With a Bitcoin transaction there is no third-party intermediary. The buyer and seller interact directly (peer to peer), but their identities are encrypted and no personal information is transferred from one to the other. However, unlike a fully anonymous transaction, there is a transaction record. A full transaction record of every Bitcoin and every Bitcoin user's encrypted identity is maintained on the public ledger. For this reason Bitcoin transactions are thought to be pseudonymous, not anonymous.

Because of the public ledger, researchers have found that, using sophisticated computer analysis, transactions involving large quantities of Bitcoin can be tracked and claim that if paired with current law enforcement tools it would be possible to gain a lot of information on the persons moving the Bitcoins.[5] Also, if Bitcoin exchanges (where large transactions are most likely to occur) are to be fully compliant with the bank secrecy regulations (i.e., anti-money laundering laws) required of other financial intermediaries, Bitcoin exchanges will be required to collect personal data on their customers, limiting further the system's ability to maintain the user's pseudonymity.

## What Is the Scale of Bitcoin Use?

Despite significant growth since its inception, Bitcoins scale of use remains that of a "niche" currency. In mid-November 2013, the total number of Bitcoins in circulation globally is approaching 12 million, up about 2 million coins from a year earlier. With its recent market price of over $1,000, Bitcoin's current market capitalization (price x number of coins in circulation) exceeds $20 billion. However, large swings in the price of Bitcoin have caused that market capitalization to exhibit similarly large changes during the year. As recently as July 2013, with Bitcoin exchanging at the much lower price of around $65, the market capitalization was below $800 million. During 2013, Bitcoin daily transaction volume fluctuated in a range of between $20 million and $40 million, representing about 40,000 daily transactions.[6]

For comparison, in September 2013 the U.S. money supply (the sum of currency, demand deposits, saving deposits including money market saving accounts) was about $10.8 trillion (about 1,000 times larger.)[7] The credit card company Visa reports that for the year ending June 2013 its total dollar volume was $6.9 trillion, with an average number of daily individual transactions of near 24 million.[8] In 2012, *daily* transactions in dollars on global foreign exchange markets averaged over $4 trillion.[9]

## Would Bitcoins Affect the Fed's Conduct of Monetary Policy?

The Federal Reserve conducts monetary policy to affect the flow of money and credit to the economy in order to achieve stable prices, maximum employment, and financial market stability. At Bitcoin's current scale of use, it is likely too small to significantly affect the Fed's ability to conduct monetary policy and achieve those three goals. However, if the scale of use were to grow substantially larger, there could be reason for some concern. *Conceptually*, Bitcoin could have an impact on the conduct of monetary policy to the extent that it would (1) substantially affect the quantity of money or (2) influence the velocity (rate of circulation) of money through the economy by reducing the demand for dollars.

Regarding the money supply, if Bitcoin transactions occur on a *pre-paid* basis whereby Bitcoins enter into circulation when dollars are exchanged and then are withdrawn from circulation when exchanged back to dollars, the net effect on the money supply would be small.

Regarding the velocity of money, if the increase in the use of Bitcoin leads to a decrease in need for holding dollars, it would increase the dollar's velocity of circulation and tend to increase the money supply associated with any given amount of base money (currency in circulation plus bank reserves held with the Fed). In this case, for the Fed to maintain the same degree of monetary accommodation, it would need to undertake a compensating tightening of monetary policy. At a minimum, a substantial use of Bitcoins could make the measurement of velocity more uncertain, and judging the appropriate stance of monetary policy uncertain.

Also, a substantial decrease in the use of dollars would also tend to reduce the size of the Fed's balance sheet and introduce another factor into its consideration of how to affect short-term interest rates (the instrument for implementing monetary policy). However, the Fed's ability to conduct monetary policy rests on its ability to increase or decrease the reserves of the banking system through open market operations. So long as there is a sizable demand by banks for liquid dollar-denominated reserves, the Fed would likely continue to be able to influence interest rates and conduct monetary policy.[10][11]

Again, any sizable effect on the U.S. monetary system is predicated on Bitcoin's scale of use becoming substantially greater than it is at present. An important force that is likely to hinder such growth in Bitcoin use is the strong preference for dollar use generated by what economists call *network externalities* (i.e., the value of a product or service is dependent on the number of others using it). Network externalities create a self-generating demand for a dominant currency. The more often a currency is used as a medium of exchange, the more liquid it becomes and the lower are the costs of transacting in it, leading, in turn, to its becoming even more attractive to new users. Network externalities create a tendency toward having one dominant currency and confer a substantial *incumbency advantage* to the dollar in both domestic and international use. The legal tender status of the dollar, discussed below, reinforces this advantage.[12]

The U.S. economy reaps considerable benefit from having a single well-defined and stable monetary unit to work as a medium of exchange and unit of account to facilitate its vast number of daily economic transactions. If greater use of Bitcoin (and other cryptocurrencies) leads to multiple monetary units, these benefits could be threatened, particularly if these new currencies continue to exhibit a high degree of price volatility. (Price volatility is discussed more fully below.)

# REASONS FOR AND AGAINST WIDER USE OF BITCOIN

## Why Would One Want to Use Bitcoins?

Bitcoin purportedly offers three potential benefits to users: lower transaction costs, increased privacy, and no erosion of purchasing power due to inflation.

### *Lower Transaction Costs for Electronic Economic Exchanges*

Because there is no third-party intermediary, Bitcoin transactions are purported to be substantially less expensive for users than those using traditional payments systems such as Paypal and traditional credit cards, which charge merchants significant fees for their role as trusted third party intermediary to validate electronic transactions. In addition, Bitcoin sales are *nonreversible*, which removes the possibility for misuse of consumer charge-backs, which merchants find costly. Merchants would presumably pass at least some of these savings on to the customer. While there is considerable anecdotal evidence that this is true, there are no comprehensive data on the size of Bitcoin's transaction cost advantage.

Some of the transaction cost advantage could be offset by the slow speed at which Bitcoin transactions currently occur, which, depending on the size of the transaction, can take a minimum of 10 minutes or as long as an hour.[13]

In addition, Bitcoin's advantage in transaction cost could be offset by the substantial volatility of Bitcoin's price. A rising dollar price of Bitcoin is likely to deter potential buyers who would expect to see their purchasing power be greater in the future. A falling Bitcoin price is likely to deter potential sellers who would expect to see their potential sales receipts be greater in the future.

### Increased Privacy

Those who seek a heightened degree of privacy may find more comfort using Bitcoins for their (legal) commercial and financial transactions. The risk of identity theft may also be less, and some may find the removal of government from a monetary system attractive. However, as discussed above, Bitcoin transactions do not have the anonymity afforded by cash transactions, as there is a permanent and complete historical record of Bitcoin amounts and encrypted identities for all transactions on the Bitcoin system that is potentially traceable.

### No Erosion of Purchasing Power by Inflation

Inflation is defined as a broad increase in the prices of goods and services. This is equivalent to saying that there is a fall in the value of the circulating currency. That fall in value means that each unit of the currency is exchangeable for a reduced amount of goods and services. Inflation is commonly thought to be a monetary phenomenon in which the supply of the currency outpaces the demand for the currency causing its unit value (in terms of what it can buy) to fall.

Most often governments (or their central bank) regulate the supply of money and credit and most often some degree of mismanagement of this government function is at the root of a persistent high inflation problem. In the case of Bitcoin, however, there is no government or central bank regulating the supply of Bitcoins. The supply of Bitcoins is programmed to grow at a steady rate regulated by the degree of mining activity (a process likely linked to a growing demand for Bitcoin) and then is capped at a fixed amount.

Inflation could occur if the demand for Bitcoin decreases relative to the fixed supply. Inflation could also occur if the Bitcoin network develops fractional reserve banking (i.e., banks that hold only a fraction of their deposits in reserve and lend out the rest), which would also be a vehicle that effectively increases the supply of circulating Bitcoins. If these digital banks move to a situation where held reserves stabilize, this source of inflation would diminish.

## What Factors Might Deter Widespread Bitcoin Use?

There are a number of factors that could discourage widespread use of Bitcoin.

### Not Legal Tender

The dollar is legal tender and by law can be used to extinguish public or private debts. A creditor is required to accept legal tender for the settlement of a debt. At a minimum, the payment of taxes forces U.S. individuals to hold dollars. Arguably, for many, such a government endorsement is comforting and creates a strong underlying demand for the dollar. By contrast, a currency like Bitcoin that is linked to a complex computer program that many do not understand and that operates without accountability to any controlling entity, could be an unattractive vehicle for holding wealth for many people.

### Does Not Enjoy the Dollar's Network Externalities

As noted above, the attractiveness of using a dollar is dependent on the number of people already using it. Thus widespread use of the dollar encourages its continued use and is an impediment (although not an insurmountable barrier) to the use of other currencies, including Bitcoins.

### Price Volatility Discourages Its Use as Medium of Exchange

Bitcoin's price has been volatile since its creation in 2009, subject to sharp appreciations and precipitous depreciations in value. However, 2013 has seen a much higher level of price fluctuation. During March and April of 2013, Bitcoin's dollar exchange rate moved from about $50 up to $350, and back to near $70. Bitcoin's price has moved up even more sharply during the fall of

2013, rising from near $50 in September to above $1,200 by early December, and down to near $800 by mid-December. This is a price pattern more typical of a commodity than a currency to be used as a medium of exchange, and suggests the market for Bitcoin is currently being driven by speculative investors, not a growing demand for Bitcoin due to increased transactions by traditional merchants and consumers.

The problem with having the Bitcoin network dominated by speculators is that it gives users an incentive to hoard Bitcoins rather than spend them—just the opposite of what would need to happen to make a currency a successful medium of exchange such as the dollar. [14]

Speculation could be more likely to dominate the market for Bitcoins because its value cannot be anchored to some underlying 'fundamental' such as an amount of some physical commodity such as gold, the value of an earnings stream that undergirds the price of a company's stock, or the perceived basic soundness and stability of an economy and its governing institutions (as is, arguably, true for the dollar).

## The System's Long-Term Deflationary Bias Will Discourage Its Use as Currency

Because the supply is capped in the long run, widespread use of Bitcoin would mean that the demand for Bitcoin would likely outstrip supply, causing Bitcoin's price to steadily increase. The corollary of that increase is that the Bitcoin price of goods and services would steadily fall causing deflation. Faced with deflation, there is a strong incentive to hoard Bitcoins and not spend them, causing the current level of transactions to fall. [15]

If generalized to an economy-wide phenomenon deflation could cause slower than normal economic growth and higher than normal unemployment.

This possible outcome highlights the likely importance of the economy's principal currency being *elastic,* its supply increasing and decreasing to meet the changing needs of the economy, and of the important role of the central bank in implementing such a monetary policy. The perils of an inelastic currency were evident, for a period from about 1880 to 1914, when the United States monetary system operated under a gold standard. At this time, the deflationary bias of an inelastic supply of gold led to elevated real interest rates, caused periodic banking panics, and produced increased instability of output. The Federal Reserve was created in 1913 to provide an elastic currency. In particular, the generally good economic performance of the post-war era speaks to the benefits of having a central bank to administer an elastic currency, not only to meet the changing transaction needs of the economy, but also to proactively use monetary policy to stabilize output and inflation.

### *Bitcoins Networks Security Is Uncertain*

While counterfeiting is purportedly not possible, Bitcoin exchanges and wallet services have at times struggled with security. Cash and traditional electronic payment systems also have periodic security problems, but a high incidence of security problems on a system trying to establish itself and gain customer confidence could be more damaging. Some notable examples of security breaches on the Bitcoin network have included the following:

- Hackers mounted a massive series of distributed denial-of-service (DDoS) attacks against the most popular Bitcoin exchange, Mt.Gox, in 2013.[16]
- In late August 2012, an operation titled Bitcoin Savings and Trust was shut down by the owner, allegedly leaving around 5.6 million USD in bitcoin-based debts.[17]
- In September 2012, Bitfloor, a Bitcoin exchange, reported being hacked, with 24,000 Bitcoins (roughly equivalent to 250,000 USD) stolen. As a result, Bitfloor temporarily suspended operations.[18]
- On April 3, 2013, Instawallet, a web-based wallet provider, was hacked, resulting in the theft of over 35,000 Bitcoins. With a price of 129.90 USD per b\Bitcoin at the time, or nearly 4.6 million USD in total, Instawallet suspended operations.[19]
- On August 11 2013, the Bitcoin Foundation announced that a bug in software within the Android operating system had been exploited to steal from users' wallets. [20]
- October 23 and 26, 2013, a Bitcoin bank, operated from Australia but stored on servers in the USA, was hacked, with a loss of 4,100 Bitcoins, or over 1 million AUD. [21]

## LEGAL AND REGULATORY ISSUES

## Legal Considerations Generally

In order to provide some information on recent efforts by federal, state, and international authorities to study, monitor, or regulate digital currencies, this section of the report (1) identifies the clause in the U.S. Constitution giving power to Congress over money; (2) describes some of the recent federal, state, and international activities and studies dealing with digital money; and (3) identifies some of the federal laws that might be implicated or that have been used with respect to digital money.

In providing this information, we have identified some federal statutes and regulatory regimes that may have some applicability to digital currency, although none contains explicit language to that effect or explicitly mentions currency not issued by a government authority. Some federal statutes, because of their broad coverage, are likely to be held by courts to apply in connection with digital currency. For example, courts are likely to hold that the federal criminal mail and wire fraud statutes apply to fraudulent schemes designed to result in monetary losses in connection with buying, selling, or trading digital currencies.[22] Federal statutes providing consumer protection with respect to consumer financial transactions, however, such as the Truth in Lending Act[23] and the Truth in Savings Act,[24] include no language specifically referencing digital currency transactions.[25]

## Power of Congress under Article I of the U.S. Constitution

One of the direct powers of Congress under the U.S. Constitution, the grant of authority "to coin Money" and "regulate the Value thereof,"[26] appears to provide sufficient authority for extensive oversight and control of digital money. The Supreme Court has interpreted this clause broadly. It has been upheld to authorize legislation chartering the First Bank of the United States and giving it power to issue circulating notes.[27] Legislation requiring U.S. Treasury notes to be treated as legal tender for antecedent debts[28] and legislation that abrogated gold clauses in private contracts[29] have also been upheld on the basis of this clause of the Constitution. The breadth of the power can be discerned from a statement of the Court in the Legal Tender Cases when the Court opined that "[e]very contract for the payment of money simply is necessarily subject to the constitutional power of the government over the currency, whatever that power may be, and the obligation of the parties is therefore assumed with reference to that power."[30]

# Recent Activity

This section provides a brief survey of some of the concerns and activities of federal, state, and international governmental entities with respect to the emergence of digital currencies.

### Recent Legislative Activity: Congress

In Congress, interest in virtual currencies is at the exploratory stage. The Senate Finance Committee directed the Government Accountability Office (GAO) to review any tax requirements and compliance risks implicated and to assess the Internal Revenue Service (IRS) efforts at informing the public in view of the offshore and internet sources of these currencies. On May 13, 2013, GAO released a survey[31] describing the types of virtual currencies, the inadequacy of available data on them, and the extent of IRS efforts. It noted that IRS guidance on virtual currencies[32] concentrates on currencies used in virtual communities, such as Linden Dollars in Second Life, and overlooks currencies, such as Bitcoin, that can be used in the real economy. GAO also notes that the tax code lacks clarity about how virtual currency is to be treated for reporting purposes. Is it property, barter, foreign currency, or a financial instrument?

The Senate Homeland Security and Governmental affairs Committee has begun to look into how federal agencies are confronting the rise of virtual currencies. On August 12, 2013, the Committee's Chairman and ranking Member sent letters[33] to several federal agencies, including the Departments of Justice (DOJ), the Treasury, and Homeland Security; the Securities and Exchange Commission (SEC); the Commodity Futures Trading Commission (CFTC); and the Federal Reserve, seeking information on their virtual currency policies, initiatives, activities, guidelines, or plans regarding virtual or digital currency. The committee envisions a government-wide approach to the threats and promises of digital currency.

### Federal Reserve and European Central Bank Studies

At least one Federal Reserve economist is studying digital currencies and Bitcoin, in particular.[34] On the international front, the European Central Bank released a study[35] of virtual currencies that assesses both the prospects for growth and some of the potential problems that might accompany widespread use.

*Federal Regulatory Activity*

Federal regulatory activity includes guidance[36] issued by Treasury's Financial Crimes Enforcement Network (FINCEN) and a Winkelvoss Bitcoin Trust registration statement[37] filed with the Securities and Exchange (SEC) Commission. In addition, the SEC published an advisory[38] for investors on the threat of virtual currency scams on the Internet, filed a criminal fraud complaint[39] charging a Bitcoin exchange with engaging in a ponzi scheme, and successfully convinced a federal district court that Bitcoins are money. The court reasoned that because Bitcoins are used as money to purchase goods or services and can be exchanged for conventional currencies, they are money, and, thus, a contract for the investment of Bitcoins is an "investment contract," and, therefore, a security under federal securities law.[40] In another enforcement action, the Department of Homeland Security charged Mt. Gox, which is the Japanese-based largest Bitcoin exchange in the United States, with operating an unlicensed money services business in violation of 18 U.S.C. §1960 and seized its bank account.

*State Regulatory Activity*

State authorities moving in the direction of regulating virtual currencies are sometimes discovering problems in applying existing laws to the technological currencies. New York's Superintendent of Financial Services is investigating whether new regulation is needed and has issued subpoenas seeking information on a raft of virtual currencies.[41] California's Department of Business Oversight may have misdirected a cease and desist order to the Bitcoin Foundation because the Foundation confines itself to advocacy work.

## APPLICABILITY OF SELECTED LAWS TO DIGITAL CURRENCY

## Counterfeiting Criminal Statutes

The basic governmental interest in enacting laws against counterfeiting obligations of the United States is protecting the value of the dollar and the monetary system. Under title 18 U.S.C. §§470- 477 and 485-489 counterfeiting and forging of U.S. coins, currency, and obligations is subject to criminal sanctions, and under 18 U.S.C. §§478-483, criminal sanctions are prescribed for counterfeiting foreign coins, currency, and obligations. None of these statutes, however, applies expressly to a currency that exists only on the Internet and in computers in a digital form. Although the usual prosecution under these statutes involves attempts to replicate Federal Reserve notes or coins produced by the U.S. Mint, at least one case involved a conviction for issuing and circulating Liberty Dollars, designed as similar to but distinguishable from U.S. dollars and intended to "limit reliance on, and to compete with, United States currency."[42] Whether a digital currency, even if it is designed to attack the value of U.S. legal tender, could be prosecuted under the current language of these statutes is not clear.[43]

## The Stamp Payments Act of 1862, 18 U.S.C. §337

The Stamp Payments Act makes it a crime to issue, circulate, or pay out "any note, check, memorandum, token or other obligation, for a less sum than $1, intended to circulate as money or to be received or used in lieu of lawful money of the United States." This law was enacted in 1862 to protect postage stamps from competition by private tokens. Congress had approved stamps as currency for fractions of $1 because metal coins were being hoarded and were virtually out of circulation.[44] It does not seem likely that a currency[45] that has no physicality would be held to be covered by this statute even though it circulates on the internet on a worldwide basis and is used for some payments of less than $1. The language of the statute, "not, check, memorandum, token," seems to contemplate a concrete object rather than a computer file; moreover, a digital currency such as Bitcoin, without a third-party issuer, cannot be said to be an obligation. However, there are some arguments that could be made, particularly should a digital currency become pervasive enough to be considered a possible competitor to U.S. official currency.[46]

## The Electronic Fund Transfer Act, 15 U.S.C. §§1693 et seq.

The Electronic Fund Transfer Act (EFTA) establishes a framework for transfers of money electronically, but its coverage is limited in such a way that it appears not to be applicable to a digital currency in transactions involving no depository institution. EFTA specifically applies to transfers of funds initiated by electronic means from a consumer's account held at a financial institution. It covers transfers "initiated through an electronic terminal, telephonic instrument, or computer."[47] Its application is limited to deposit accounts "established primarily for personal, family, or household purposes,"[48] "held by a financial institution,"[49] with "financial institution" limited to banks, thrifts, savings associations, and credit unions.[50]

## Federal Tax Law

Digital currencies have characteristics of traditional tax haven jurisdictions: earnings are not reported to the Internal Revenue Service (IRS) and users are provided some level of anonymity. Unlike traditional tax havens, however, digital currencies are able to operate without involving a financial institution.[51] The IRS provides limited guidance on the tax consequences of activities involving the virtual world. It cautions: "[i]n general, you can receive income in the form of money, property, or services. If you receive more income from the virtual world than you spend, you may be required to report the gain as taxable income. IRS guidance also applies when you spend more in a virtual world than you receive, you generally cannot claim a loss on an income tax return."[52] The guidance is limited and does not appear to target a digital currency such as Bitcoin that is used as a medium of exchange for goods and services in the real world. A Government Accountability Office (GAO) report earlier this year found inadequate IRS efforts to address tax implications of virtual currencies not used within a virtual economy.[53] As a step to counter misinformation circulating and the possibility for growth in such currencies, rather than recommending a costly rigorous compliance approach, GAO recommended that IRS "find relatively low-cost ways to provide information to taxpayers, such as the web statement IRS developed on virtual economies, on the basic tax reporting requirements for transactions using virtual currencies developed and used outside virtual economies."[54]

## Federal Anti-Money Laundering Laws

Under the criminal anti-money laundering laws,[55] engaging in financial transactions that involve proceeds of illegal or terrorist activities or that are designed to finance such activities is prohibited. Money laundering crimes generally involve transactions processed by financial institutions, which is why the Bank Secrecy Act (BSA) imposes various recordkeeping requirements on banks and other financial institutions.[56] Under the Currency and Foreign Transaction Reporting Act[57] component of the BSA, financial institutions must file reports of cash transactions exceeding amounts set by the Secretary of the Treasury in regulations, and file suspicious activity reports (SARs) for transactions meeting a certain monetary threshold or intended to evade reporting requirements. Financial institutions, as required by the Secretary of the Treasury, must also develop and follow anti-money laundering programs and customer identification programs. All of these requirements apply to "money services businesses" (MSBs), a category of financial institution which must register with the Department of the Treasury.[58] MSBs include a variety of businesses, including dealers in foreign exchange, check cashers, traveler's check issuers, providers of prepaid access cards, and money transmitters.[59] These entities must register with the Department of the Treasury and comply with BSA requirements. On March 18, 2013, FINCEN issued interpretative guidance[60] requiring Bitcoin exchanges— individuals and businesses that change Bitcoins into U.S. or foreign currency into Bitcoins—to register as money services businesses pursuant to the BSA.

## Federal Securities Regulation

Securities regulation may focus on two different legal issues involving Bitcoins—investments purchased with Bitcoins and investing in Bitcoins.

### Investments Purchased with Bitcoins

The United States District Court for the Eastern District of Texas held in August 2013 that it had subject matter jurisdiction over possible fraud in investments purchased with Bitcoins because of its determination that investments purchased with Bitcoins are securities.[61] The Securities and Exchange Commission (SEC) alleged that the defendant had violated provisions of the Securities Act of 1933[62] and the Securities Exchange Act of 1934[63] and had conducted a kind of Ponzi scheme. According to the facts stated by the SEC, the defendant, Trendon T. Shavers, who was the founder and operator of Bitcoin Savings and Trust (BTCST), solicitations aimed at enticing lenders to invest in Bitcoin-related investment opportunities." Shavers had advertised that he sold Bitcoins and that he would pay an investor up to 1% interest daily until the investor withdrew the funds or until BTCST could no longer be profitable. Investors lost a considerable amount of money, and the SEC brought suit. Shavers defended that the BTCST investments were not securities under federal securities laws because Bitcoins are not money and are not regulated by the United States. Shavers seemed also to argue that, because the investments were not securities, the court had no jurisdiction over a lawsuit alleging violations of the federal securities laws. The SEC argued that the BTCST investments were investment contracts, thus bringing them within the definition of "securities" and therefore subject to regulation by the SEC.

The court held that it did have jurisdiction over the case because of its determination that investments purchased with Bitcoins are securities. 15 U.S.C. section 77b defines a "security" in a very broad way as "any note, stock, treasury stock, security future, security-based swap, bond ... [or] investment contract." Cases such as SEC v. W.J. Howey & Co[64] and Long v. Schultz Cattle Co.[65] have set out a kind of template for an investment contract: An investment contract involves (1) an investment of money (2) in a common enterprise (3) with the expectation of profits from the efforts of a promoter or a third party. Thus, according to the court, it had to determine whether the BTCST investments were an investment of money. The court found that, because Bitcoins can be used to purchase goods or services and even used to pay for individual living expenses, they are a "currency or form of money" and that "investors wishing to invest in BTCST provided an investment of money." The court also found that there was a common enterprise because the investors were dependent upon Shavers's expertise in Bitcoin markets and that Shavers promised a significant return on their investments. Finally, the Eastern District of Texas found that the third prong of the investment contract template was met because the BTCST investors had an expectation of deriving profits from their investments. Because it found that the BTCST investments satisfied the investment contract definition, the court held that it had subject matter jurisdiction over possible fraud in investments purchased with Bitcoins.

### Investing in Bitcoins

Investing in bitcoins may trigger regulation by the SEC. For example, it has been reported that Cameron and Tyler Winkelvoss are forming a public exchange-traded fund (ETF) for bitcoins and have filed paperwork with the SEC.[66] The ETF may be traded on a major exchange and open to retail investors. According to the SEC's website, an ETF is often registered as an open-end investment company or unit investment trust under the Investment Company Act of 1940. The regulatory requirements for ETFs include the following:

> As investment companies, ETFs are subject to the regulatory requirements of the federal securities laws as well as certain exemptions

that are necessary for ETFs to operate under those laws. Together, the federal securities laws and the relevant exemptions apply requirements that are designed to protect investors from various risks and conflicts associated with investing in ETFs.

For example, ETFs, like mutual funds, are subject to statutory limitations on their use of leverage and transactions with affiliates. ETFs also are subject to specific reporting requirements and disclosure obligations relating to investment objectives, risks, expenses, and other information in their registration statements and periodic reports.

In addition, ETFs are subject to oversight by boards of directors.[67]

## Commodity Futures Trading Commission Regulation

The Commodity Futures Trading Commission (CFTC) has authority to regulate commodities futures and their markets and certain foreign exchange instruments. It is possible that CFTC could conclude that a digital currency such as Bitcoins falls within the Commodity Exchange Act's (CEA's) definition of "commodity," which includes a catch-all phrase—"and all other goods and articles."[68] There is also the possibility that the CFTC could include such a digital currency within its foreign exchange regulations because the CEA does not define "foreign currency" or "foreign exchange," although it covers and defines "foreign-exchange forwards" and "foreign-exchange swaps."[69]

# INTERNATIONAL LEGAL ISSUES

Because digital currency knows no national boundaries, it may require an international solution and, thus, has drawn the attention of international regulators. Traditional payment systems which involve monetary systems are set up in statutes and regulations and overseen by central banks and transactions processed by banks and other authorized or chartered financial institutions. With virtual currencies, however, no laws and regulations define the duties and obligations of parties, provide for finality of settlement, resolution of disputes, or supervision of services provided. One recent study of digital currencies by the European Central Bank is premised on the possibility that growth of digital currencies will carry with it a need for international cooperation in developing a regulatory framework.[70] According to the report, the current level of virtual currencies poses little risk to price stability; there are, however, risks to users and a potential for criminal schemes.[71] According to the report, neither the European Monetary Directive nor the European Payment Services Directive clearly applies to virtual currencies such as Bitcoin.[72]

## Concern About International Monetary Fund Authority

One issue that has received some attention is the ability of the International Monetary Fund (IMF) to defend a traditional currency of one of its member countries from a speculative attack involving a digital currency such as Bitcoin since the IMF's Articles of Agreement do not explicitly permit it to acquire a currency not issued by one of its members. There is at least one commentary[73] examining possible options for amending or reinterpreting the IMF's authority.

## End Notes

[1] On November 18, the Senate committee on Homeland Security and Governmental Affairs held a hearing on: Beyond Silk Road: Potential Risks, Threats, and Promises, available at http://www.hsgac.senate.gov/hearings/beyond-silkroad-potential-risks-threats-and-promises-of-virtual-currencies. On November 19, the Senate Committee on Banking, Housing, and Urban Affairs held a hearing on: The Current and Future Impact of Virtual Currencies, available at http://www.banking.senate.gov/public/index.cfm? FuseAction=Hearings.Hearing&Hearing_ID=955322cc-d648-4a00- a41f-c23be8ff4cad.

[2] General background discussions about Bitcoin can be found at Bitcoin, available at http://bitcoin.org/en/; Jerry Brito and Andrea Castillo, Bitcoin: a Primer for Policymakers, Mercatus Center, George Mason University, 2013, available at http://mercatus.org/publication/bitcoin-primer-policymakers; and Federal Reserve Bank of Chicago, Chicago Fed Letter, Bitcoin: A Primer, 2013, available at http://www.chicagofed.org/digital_assets/publications/chicago_fed_letter/ 2013/cfldecember2013_317.pdf.

[3] The current price of a Bitcoin can be obtained from Bitcoin-Charts available at http://bitcoincharts.com/.

[4] Joshua Brustein, "Bitcoin May Not Be Anonymous After All," Bloomberg Business Week, August 27, 2013, available at http://www.businessweek.com/articles/2013-08-27/bitcoin-may-not-be-so-anonymous-after-all.

[5] Sarah Meiklejohn, Marjori Pomarole, Grant Jordan, Kirill Levchenko, Damon McCoy, Geoffrey M. Voelker, and Stefan Savage, "A Fist Full of Bitcoins: Characterizing Payments Among Men with No Name," University of California, San Diego, December 2013, available at http://cseweb.ucsd.edu/~smeiklejohn/.

[6] Bitcoin data from Bitcoin Charts available at http://bitcoincharts.com/.

[7] Board of Governors of the Federal Reserve System, Money Stock Measures(H.6), available at http://www.federalreserve.gov/releases/h6/current/default.htm.

[8] Visa, Inc., Fact Sheet, available at http://corporate.visa.com/_media/visa-fact-sheet.pdf.

[9] Bank for International Settlements, "Foreign Exchange Turnover in April 2013: Preliminary Global Results," Triennial Central Bank Survey, September 2013, https://www.bis.org/publ/rpfx13fx.pdf.

[10] See also: European Central Bank, Virtual Currency Schemes, October 2012, pp33-39, available at http://www.ecb.europa.eu/pub/pdf/other/virtualcurrencyschemes201210en.pdf.

[11] In a recent letter to the Senate Committee on Homeland Security and Governmental Affairs, Fed Chairman Bernanke noted that virtual currencies have the potential to be beneficial, but also carry risks, and while not a direct regulatory responsibility, are monitored by the Fed. He did not express any concern about virtual currencies hindering the Fed's ability to conduct monetary policy. Available at http://online.wsj.com/public/resources /documents/ VCurrenty111813.pdf.

[12] Varian, Hal R., 2003, "Economics of Information Technology," in "Academic Papers and Books, 2004 and Earlier Non-technical papers," available at http://www.sims.berkeley.edu/~hal.

[13] See Data on transaction times at Blockchain, available at http://blockchain.info/charts/avg-confirmation-time.

[14] Felix Salmon, "The Bitcoin Bubble and the Future of Currency," Medium, April 2013, available at https://medium.com/money-banking/2b5ef79482cb.

[15] Dan Kervick, "Bitcoin's Deflationary Weirdness," New Economic Perspectives, April 2013, available at http://neweconomicperspectives.org/2013/04/talking-bitcoin.html.

[16] Mitt Clinch, "Bitcoin Hacked: Price Stumbles After Buying Frenzy," CNBC, April 4, 2013, available at http://www.cnbc.com/id/100615508.

[17] Adrianne Jeffries, "Suspected Multi-Million Dollar Bitcoin Pyramid Scheme Shuts Down, Investors Revolt," The Verge, August 27, 2012, available at http://www.theverge.com/ 2012/8/27/3271637/bitcoin-savings-trust-pyramidscheme-shuts-down.

[18] Vitalik Burterin, "Bitfloor Hacked, $250,000 Missing," Bitcoin Magazine, Sept 4, 2012, available at http://bitcoinmagazine.com/2139/bitfloor-hacked-250000-missing/.

[19] Joe Weisenthal, "Bitcoin Service Instawallet: We've Been Hacked and are Suspending Service Indefinitely," Business Insider, April 3, 2013, available at http://www.business insider.com/instawallet-suspended-2013-4.

[20] Richard Chirgwen, "Android Bug Batters Bitcoin Wallets," The Register, August 12, 2013, available at http://www.theregister.co.uk/2013/08/12/android_bug_batters_bitcoin_wallets/.

[21] Ben Grubb, "Australian Bitcoin Bank Hacked: $1 Million + Stolen," Brisbane Times, November 8, 2013, available at http://www.brisbanetimes.com.au/it-pro/security-it/australian-bitcoin-bank-hacked-1m-stolen-20131108-hv2iv.html.

[22] These include 18 U.S.C. §§1341 (mail fraud) and 1343 (wire fraud). The wire fraud statute, for example, applies to "[w]hoever, having devised or intending to devise any scheme or artifice to defraud, or for obtaining money or property by means of false or fraudulent pretenses, representations, or promises, transmits or causes to be transmitted by means of wire, radio, or television communication in interstate or foreign commerce, any writings, signs, signals, pictures, or sounds for the purpose of executing such scheme or artifice." Regulation Z, 12 C.F.R. 226, implementing the Truth in Lending Act (TILA) is premised on credit transactions, interest, and fees in terms of U.S. money. At present it is a matter of pure speculation as to whether the Consumer Financial Protection Board (CFPB), the agency charged with implementing TILA, could reasonably interpret the statute, given its

language, structure, and legislative history, as a basis for issuing regulations to cover transactions in digital money.

[23] 15 U.S.C. §§1601 et seq.

[24] 12 U.S.C. §§4301-4313. (This applies to deposits held at depository institutions, i.e., banks, thrifts, savings associations, and credit unions.).

[25] A list of the regulations implementing federal laws providing consumer protection for financial transactions can be found on the Consumer Financial Protection Bureau's website at http://www.consumerfinance.gov/regulations/#ecfr,\.

[26] U.S. Const., art. I, §8, cl. 5.

[27] McCulloch v. Maryland, 17 U.S. (4 Wheat.) 316 (1819); Veazie Bank v. Fenno, 75 U.S. (8 Wall.) 533 (1869).

[28] Legal Tender Cases (Knox v. Lee), 79 U.S. (12 Wall.) 457(1871); Juilliard v. Greenman, 110 U.S. 421 (1884).

[29] Norman v. Baltimore & Ohio R.R., 294 U.S. 240 (1935).

[30] Legal Tender Cases (Knox v. Lee), 79 U.S. (12 Wall.) 457, 549 (1871).

[31] U.S. Government Accountability Office, "Virtual Economies and Currencies: Additional IRS Guidance Could Reduce Tax Compliance Risks" (May 2013).

[32] Internal Revenue Service, "Tax Consequences of Virtual World Transactions," http://www.irs.gov/Businesses/SmallBusinesses-&-Self-Employed/Tax-Consequences-of-Virtual-World-Transactions.

[33] http://www.hsgac.senate.gov/reports/letters

[34] François R. Velde, "Bitcoin: A primer," Chicago Fed Letter (December 2013). http://www.chicagofed.org/digital_assets/publications/chicago_fed_letter/2013/cfldecember2013_317.pdf.

[35] European Central Bank, "Virtual Currency Schemes," (October 2012). http://www.google.com/url?sa=t&rct=j&q=&esrc=s&frm=1&source=web&cd=1&ved=0CCsQFjAA&url=http%3A%2F%2Fwww.ecb.europa.eu%2Fpub%2Fpdf%2Fother%2Fvirtualcurrencyschemes201210en.pdf&ei=UiCUp_HGoqqsQSJ0YCICQ&usg=AFQjCNHPyKEw4gnOcQ27d-znAvyPmONT3g&bvm=bv.56146854,d.cWc.

[36] U.S. Department of the Treasury, Financial Crimes Enforcement Network, "Application of FinCEN's Regulations to Persons Administering, Exchanging, or Using Virtual Currencies," (March 18, 2013), http://www.fincen.gov/ statutes_regs/guidance/html/FIN-2013-G001.html.

[37] Form S-1 Registration Statement, Winkelvoss Bitcoin Trust. http://www.sec.gov/ Archives/edgar/data/1579346/ 000119312513279830/d562329ds1.htm.

[38] U.S. Securities and Exchange Commission Press Release 2013-132, "SEC Charges Texas Man with Running Bitcoin-Denominated Ponzi Scheme," (July 23, 2013). http://www.sec.gov/News/PressRelease/Detail/PressRelease/ 1370539730583.

[39] http://www.sec.gov/litigation/complaints/2013/comp-pr2013-132.pdf.

[40] Securities and Exchange Commission v. Shavers, 2013 WL4028182, No. 4:13-CV-416 (E.D. Tex. Aug. 6, 2013). This appears to be the first ruling addressing the question of whether digital currency issued without the backing of a government or other official entity is to be legally considered money.

[41] New York State, Department of Financial Services, "Notice of Inquiry on Virtual Currencies," August 12, 2013. http://www.dfs.ny.gov/about/press2013/memo1308121.pdf.

[42] Derek A. Dion, "Defendant Convicted of Minting His Own Currency," Press Release, U.S. Attorney's Office, Western District of North Carolina (March 18, 2011). http://www. fbi.gov/charlotte/press-releases/2011/defendantconvicted-of-minting-his-own-currency.

[43] For a discussion, see, "I'll Gladly Trade You Two Bits on Tuesday for a Byte Today: Bitcoin, Regulating Fraud in the E-conomy of Hacker Cash," 2013 University of Illinois Journal of Law, Technology and Policy (Spring 2013).

[44] For further exposition of the genesis, legislative history, and analysis of the Stamp Payments Act, including the possibility that it may apply to electronic currency, see Thomas P. Vartanian, Robert H. Ledig, and Yolanda Demianczuk, "Echoes of the Past with Implications for the Future: The Stamp Payments Act of 1862 and Electronic Commerce", 67 BNA's Banking Report (September 23, 1996).

[45] Virtual currencies, such as Linden Dollars, are not likely to conflict with this statute because they do not appear to "circulate as money or be received in lieu of lawful money," within the meaning of the statute. They circulate only in a limited environment and are redeemable only in virtual goods, and, thus, are similar to the tokens and tickets redeemable in goods and services on a limited basis that courts have found not to have been issued in violation of the Stamp Payments Act. United States v. Monongahela Bridge Co., 26 F. Cas. 1292 (W.D. Pa. 1863) (No. 15796); United States v. Roussopulous, 95 F. 977 (D. Minn. 1899).

[46] See Vartanian, et al., supra, n. 8, and Reuben Grinberg, "Bitcoin: An Innovative Digital Currency, 5 Hastings Science & Technology Law Journal 159 (2012).

[47] 15 U.S.C. §1693a(6).

[48] 15 U.S.C. §1693a(2).

[49] 15 U.S.C. §1693a(2).

[50] 15 U.S.C. §1693a(11).

[51] For further information see, Marian, Omri, "Are Cryptocurrencies Super Tax Havens?," 112 Michigan Law Review First Impressions 38 (2013).

[52] Internal Revenue Service, "Tax Consequences of Virtual World Transactions," http://www.irs. gov/Businesses/SmallBusinesses-&-Self-Employed/Tax-Consequences-of-Virtual-World-Transactions.

[53] U.S. Government Accountability Office, "Virtual Economies and Currencies: Additional IRS Guidance Could Reduce Tax Compliance Risk," (May 2013).

[54] U.S. Government Accountability Office, "Virtual Economies and Currencies: Additional IRS Guidance Could Reduce Tax Compliance Risk," 17 (May 2013).

[55] 18 U.S.C. §§1956 and 1957.

[56] Titles I and II of P.L. 91-508, including 12 U.S.C. §§1829b, and 1951-1959; 31 U.S.C. §§5311 et seq.

[57] 31 U.S.C. §§5311 et seq.

[58] Bank Secrecy Act requirements for money services businesses are listed on the Financial Crimes Enforcement Network's website at http://www.fincen.gov/financial _institutions/ msb/msbrequirements.html.

[59] 31 C.F.R. §1010.100(ff).

[60] U.S. Department of the Treasury, Financial Crimes Enforcement Network, "Application of FinCEN's Regulations to Persons Administering, Exchanging, or Using Virtual Currencies," (March 18, 2013), http://www.fincen.gov/ statutes_regs/guidance/html/FIN-2013-G001.html.

[61] Securities and Exchange Commission v. Shavers, No. 4:13-CV-416 (E.D. Tex. Aug. 6, 2013).

[62] 15 U.S.C. §§77a et seq.

[63] 15 U.S.C. §§78a et seq.

[64] 328 U.S. 293 (1946).

[65] 881 F.2d 129 (5th Cir. 1989).

[66] http://qz/99632/winkelvoss-bitcoin-etf-risk-factors.

[67] sec.gov/investor/alerts/etfs.pdf.

[68] 7 U.S.C. §1a(9). It reads: The term "commodity" means wheat, cotton, rice, corn, oats, barley, rye, flaxseed, grain sorghums, mill feeds, butter, eggs, Solanum tuberosum (Irish potatoes), wool, wool tops, fats and oils (including lard, tallow, cottonseed oil, peanut oil, soybean oil, and all other fats and oils), cottonseed meal, cottonseed, peanuts, soybeans, soybean meal, livestock, livestock products, and frozen concentrated orange juice, and all other goods and articles, except onions (as provided by section 13–1 of this title) and motion picture box office receipts (or any index, measure, value, or data related to such receipts), and all services, rights, and interests (except motion picture box office receipts, or any index, measure, value or data related to such receipts) in which contracts for future delivery are presently or in the future dealt in.

[69] 7 U.S.C. §§1a(24) and (25).

[70] European Central Bank, "Virtual Currency Schemes," (October 2012). http://www.ecb. europa.eu/pub/pdf/other/ virtualcurrencyschemes201210en.pdf. (Hereinafter, European Central Bank Report.)

[71] European Central Bank, "Virtual Currency Schemes," (October 2012). http://www.ecb. europa.eu/pub/pdf/other/ virtualcurrencyschemes201210en.pdf. (Hereinafter, European Central Bank Report.)

[72] European Central Bank Report, at 43. The report notes noted that there are attempts in some of the countries belonging to the European Union to develop a means of regulating such currencies. Apparently courts in France are looking into whether Bitcoin transactions are subject to electronic money regulations. See Finextra.http://www.finextra.com/ news/ fullstory.aspx?newsitemid=22921.

[73] Nicholas Plassarus, "Regulating Digital Currencies: Bringing Bitcoin within the Reach of the IMF," 14 Chicago Journal of International Law 377 (2013), https://papers.ssrn.com/sol3 /papers.cfm?abstract_id=2248419.

In: Money, Economics, and Finance. Volume 3     ISBN: 978-1-63321-505-4
Editor: Clifford Dobrowski                    © 2014 Nova Science Publishers, Inc.

*Chapter 2*

# CURRENT DEBATES OVER EXCHANGE RATES: OVERVIEW AND ISSUES FOR CONGRESS[*]

## *Rebecca M. Nelson*

### SUMMARY

Exchange rates are important in the international economy, because they affect the price of every country's imports and exports, as well as the value of every overseas investment. Following the global financial crisis of 2008-2009 and ensuing economic recession, disagreements among countries over exchange rates have become more widespread. Some policy leaders and analysts contend that there is a "currency war" now underway among certain countries.

At the heart of current disagreements is whether or not countries are using exchange rate policies to undermine free markets and intentionally push down the value of their currency in order to gain a trade advantage at the expense of other countries. A weak currency makes exports cheaper to foreigners, which can lead to higher exports and job creation in the export sector. However, if one country weakens its currency, there can be implications for other countries. In general, exporters and firms producing import-sensitive goods may find it harder to compete against countries with weak currencies. However, consumers and businesses that

---

[*] This is an edited, reformatted and augmented version of a Congressional Research Service publication, No. R43242, dated November 12, 2013.

rely on inputs from abroad may benefit when other countries have weak currencies, because imports may become cheaper.

The United States has found itself on both sides of the current debates over exchange rates. On one hand, some Members of Congress and U.S. policy experts argue that U.S. exports and U.S. jobs have been adversely affected by the exchange rate policies adopted by China, Japan, and a number of other countries. On the other hand, some emerging markets, including Brazil and Russia, have argued that expansionary monetary policies in the United States and other developed countries caused the currencies of developed countries to depreciate, hurting the competitiveness of emerging markets. More recently, however, emerging-market currencies have started to depreciate, and now there are concerns about emerging-market currencies becoming too weak relative to the currencies of some developed economies.

Through the International Monetary Fund (IMF), countries have committed to avoid "currency manipulation." There are also provisions in U.S. law to address "currency manipulation" by other countries. In the context of recent disagreements, neither the IMF nor the U.S. Treasury Department has determined any country to be manipulating its exchange rate. There are differing views on why. Some argue that countries have not engaged in policies that violate international commitments on exchange rates or triggered provisions in U.S. law relating to currency manipulation. Others argue that currency manipulation has occurred, but that estimating a currency's "true" or "fundamental" value is complicated, and that the current international financial architecture is not effective at responding to exchange rate disputes.

## Policy Options for Congress

Some Members of Congress may consider addressing exchange rate issues because they are concerned about the impact of other countries' exchange rate policies on the competitiveness of U.S. products. Recently, concerns have been raised about the impact of Japan's economic policies on the value of the yen, and the implications for the U.S. economy. However, there are a number of potential consequences from taking action on exchange rates that Congress might also want to consider. For example, U.S. imports from countries with weak currencies may be less expensive than they would be otherwise; countries may retaliate after being labeled a currency "manipulator"; and tensions over exchange rates could dissipate as the global economy strengthens.

If Members did decide to take action, they have a number of options for doing so. Options could include urging the Administration to address currency disputes at the IMF and in trade agreements, or passing legislation relating to countries determined to have undervalued exchange rates, among others. Two bills have been introduced in the 113$^{th}$ Congress related to exchange rate policies in other countries (H.R. 1276; S. 1114). Representative Levin has also released a proposal for addressing currency issues in the Trans-Pacific Partnership, a proposed free trade agreement that the United States is negotiating with Japan and 10 other Asia-Pacific countries.

## INTRODUCTION

Some policy makers and analysts allege that certain countries are using exchange rate policies to gain an "unfair" trade advantage. They maintain that some countries are purposefully using various policies to weaken the value of their currency to boost exports and create jobs, but that these policies come at the expense of other countries. Some political leaders and policy experts contend that there is a "currency war" in the global economy, as countries compete against each other to weaken the value of their currencies and boost exports.[1]

The United States has found itself on both sides of the debate. On one hand, some Members of Congress and U.S. policy experts argue that U.S. producers and U.S. jobs have been adversely affected by the exchange rate policies adopted by China, Japan, and a number of other countries. On the other hand, some emerging markets, including Brazil and Russia, have argued that expansionary monetary policies in the United States and other major developed countries have reduced the value of the dollar and other currencies, and thereby have hurt the competitiveness of emerging markets. More recently, some in the United States have started discussing pulling back expansionary monetary policies, and emerging-market currencies have started to weaken.

There are now concerns about emerging-market currencies becoming too weak relative to the currencies of some developed economies.

During the 113$^{th}$ Congress, some Members of Congress have proposed taking action on exchange rate issues:

- Legislation has been introduced aimed at countries determined to have fundamentally undervalued or misaligned exchange rates (the

Currency Reform for Fair Trade Act, H.R. 1276; the Currency Exchange Rate Oversight Reform Act of 2013, S. 1114).

- Some Members have expressed concerns about Japan's monetary policies and its effect on exchange rates, which impact the competitiveness of U.S. exports. These concerns have been raised particularly in the context of the Trans-Pacific Partnership (TPP) negotiations. TPP is a proposed regional trade agreement that the United States is negotiating with Japan and 10 other countries in the Asia-Pacific region.[2] In June 2013, 230 Representatives sent a letter to President Obama urging the Administration to address unfair exchange rate policies in the TPP, particularly with regards to Japan.[3] In September 2013, 60 Senators sent a letter to the Treasury Secretary, Jacob Lew, and the U.S. Trade Representative, Michael Froman, asking them to address currency "manipulation" in the TPP and all future free trade agreements.[4] Representative Levin released a specific proposal to address unfair exchange rate practices in the TPP in July 2013.[5]

- Some Members have also called on the Administration to address currency issues in negotiations with the European Union (EU) over a proposed free trade agreement (the Transatlantic Trade and Investment Partnership [TTIP]) and in renewal of Trade Promotion Authority (TPA).[6] TPA is the authority Congress grants to the President to enter into certain reciprocal trade agreements and to have their implementing bills considered under expedited legislative procedures when certain conditions have been met.[7] TPA expired in 2007 and some Members are looking to renew it to facilitate trade negotiations.

This report provides information on current debates over exchange rates in the global economy. It offers an overview of how exchange rates work; analyzes specific disagreements and debates; and examines existing frameworks for potentially addressing currency disputes. It also lays out some policy options available to Congress, should Members want to take action on exchange rate issues.

# THE IMPORTANCE OF EXCHANGE RATES IN THE GLOBAL ECONOMY

## What Is an Exchange Rate?

An exchange rate is the price of a country's currency relative to other currencies. In other words, it is the rate at which one currency can be converted into another currency. For example, on August 30, 2013, one U.S. dollar could be exchanged for 0.76 euros (€), 98 Japanese yen (¥), or 0.65 British pounds (£).[8] Exchange rates are expressed in terms of dollars per foreign currency, or expressed in terms of foreign currency per dollar. The exchange rate between dollars and euros on August 30, 2013, can be quoted as 1.32 $/€ or, equivalently, 0.76 €/$. Consumers use exchange rates to calculate the cost of goods produced in other countries. For example, U.S. consumers use exchange rates to calculate how much a bottle of French or Australian wine costs in U.S. dollars. Likewise, French and Australian consumers use exchange rates to calculate how much a bottle of U.S. wine costs in euros or Australian dollars. How much a currency is worth in relation to another currency is determined by the supply and demand for currencies in the foreign exchange market (the market in which foreign currencies are traded). The foreign exchange market is substantial, and has expanded in recent years. Trading in foreign exchange markets averaged $5.3 trillion per day in April 2013, up from $3.3 trillion in April 2007.[9]

The relative demand for currencies reflects the underlying demand for goods and assets denominated in that currency, and large international capital flows can have a strong influence on the demand for various currencies. The government, typically the central bank, can use policies to shape the supply of its currency in international capital markets.

---

**Different Measures of Exchange Rates**

- Nominal vs. real exchange rate: The nominal exchange rate is the rate at which two currencies can be exchanged, or how much one currency is worth in terms of another currency. The real exchange rate measures the value of a country's goods against those of another country at the prevailing nominal exchange rate. Essentially, the real exchange rate adjusts the nominal exchange rate for differences in prices (and rates of inflation) across countries.

> • Bilateral vs. effective exchange rate: The bilateral exchange rate is the value of one currency in terms of another currency. The effective exchange rate is the value of a currency against a weighted average of several currencies (a "basket" of foreign currencies). The basket can be weighted in different ways, such as by share of world trade or GDP. The Bank for International Settlements (BIS), for example, publishes data on effective exchange rates.[10]

## Impact on International Trade and Investment

### *International Trade*

Exchange rates affect the price of every export leaving a country and every import entering a country. As a result, changes in the exchange rate can impact trade flows. When the value of a country's currency falls, or depreciates, relative to another currency, its exports become less expensive to foreigners and imports from overseas become more expensive to domestic consumers.[11] These changes in relative prices can cause the level of exports to rise and the level of imports to fall.[12] For example, if the dollar depreciates against the British pound, U.S. exports become cheaper to UK consumers, and imports from the UK become more expensive to U.S. consumers. As a result, U.S. exports to the UK may rise, and U.S. imports from the UK may fall.

Likewise, when the value of a currency rises, or appreciates, the country's exports become more expensive to foreigners and imports become less expensive to domestic consumers. This can cause exports to fall and imports to rise. For example, if the dollar appreciates against the Australian dollar, U.S. exports become more expensive to Australian consumers, and imports from Australia become less expensive to U.S. consumers. Changes in prices may cause U.S. exports to Australia to fall and U.S. imports from Australia to rise.

### *International Investment*

Exchange rates impact international investment in two ways. First, exchange rates determine the value of existing overseas investments. When a currency depreciates, the value of investments denominated in that currency falls for overseas investors. Likewise, when a currency appreciates, the value of investments denominated in that currency rises for overseas investors. For example, if a U.S. investor holds a German government bond denominated in euros, and the euro depreciates, the value of the bond in U.S. dollars falls, making the investment worth less to the U.S. investor. In contrast, if the euro appreciates, the value of the German bond in U.S. dollars rises, and the investment is worth more to the U.S. investor.

Second, exchange rates impact the flow of investment across borders. Changes in the value of a currency today can shape investors' future expectations about the value of the currency, which can have substantial impacts on capital flows. If investors expect a currency to depreciate, overseas investors may be reluctant to invest in assets denominated in that currency and may want to sell assets denominated in the currency, in fear that their investments will become less valuable over time. Likewise, if a currency is expected to rise over time, assets denominated in that currency become more attractive to overseas investors. For example, a depreciating euro may deter U.S. investment in the Eurozone, while an appreciating euro may increase U.S. investment in the Eurozone.[13]

## Types of Exchange Rate Policies

There are two major ways that the price of a country's currency is determined, or types of "currency regimes." First, some governments "float" their currencies. This means they allow the price of their currency to fluctuate depending on supply and demand for currencies in foreign exchange markets. Governments with floating exchange rates do not take policy actions to influence the value of their currencies.

Second, some countries "fix" or "peg" their exchange rate. This means they fix the value of their currency to another currency (such as the U.S. dollar or euro), a group (or "basket") of currencies, or a commodity, such as gold. The government (typically the central bank) then uses various policies to control the supply and demand for the currency in foreign exchange markets to maintain the set price for the currency. Often, central banks maintain exchange rate pegs by buying and selling currency in foreign exchange markets, or "intervening" in foreign exchange markets.

There are pros and cons to having a floating or fixed exchange rate. Fixed exchange rates provide more certainty in international transactions, but they can make it more difficult for the economy to adjust to economic shocks and can make the currency more susceptible to speculative attacks. Floating exchange rates introduce more unpredictability in international transactions and may deter international trade and investment, but make it easier for the economy to adjust to changes in economic conditions.

In order to take advantage of the benefits of both fixed and floating exchange rates, many countries do not adopt a purely fixed or floating exchange rate, but choose a hybrid policy: they let the currency's value fluctuate but take action to keep the exchange rate from deviating too far from a target value or zone. The degree to which they float or peg varies. The optimal choice for any given country will depend on its characteristics, including its size and interconnectedness to the country to which it would peg its currency.

Between the end of World War II and the early 1970s, most countries, including the United States, had fixed exchange rates.[14] In the early 1970s, when international capital flows increased, the United States abandoned its peg to gold and floated the dollar. Other countries' currencies were pegged to the dollar, and after the dollar floated, some other countries decided to float their currencies as well.

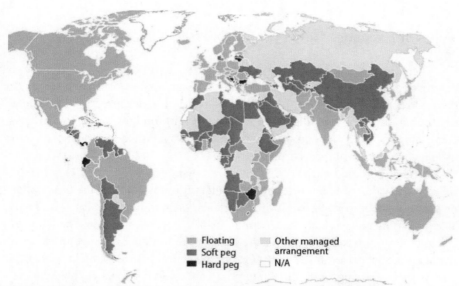

Floating       Other managed
Soft peg       arrangement
Hard peg       N/A

Source: IMF, "Annual Report on Exchange Arrangements and Exchange Restrictions,"
       2012.
Notes: See footnote 15.

Figure 1. Map of Exchange Rate Policies by Country.

In 2012, 35% of countries had floating currencies.[15] This includes several major currencies, such as the U.S. dollar, the euro, the Japanese yen, and the British pound, whose economies together account for 50% of global GDP.[16]

Many countries use policies to manage the value of their currencies, although some manage it more than others. This includes many small countries, such as Panama and Hong Kong, as well as a few larger economies, such as China, Russia, and Saudi Arabia. In 2012, 40% of countries used a "soft" peg, which let the exchange rate fluctuate within a desired range, and 13% of countries used a "hard" peg, which anchors the currency's value more strictly, including the formal adoption of a foreign currency to use as a domestic currency (for example, Ecuador has adopted the U.S. dollar as its national currency).[17] No large country uses a hard peg. **Figure 1** depicts the exchange rate policies adopted by different countries.

## Exchange Rate Misalignments

Many economists believe that exchange rate levels can differ from the underlying "fundamental" or "equilibrium" value of the exchange rate. When an actual exchange rate differs from its fundamental or equilibrium value, the currency is said to be misaligned. More specifically, when the actual exchange rate is too high, the currency is said to be overvalued; when the actual rate is too low, the currency is said to be undervalued.

Considerable debate exists about what the fundamental or equilibrium value of a currency is and how to define or calculate currency misalignment.[18] For example, some economists believe that a currency is misaligned when the exchange rate set by the government, or the official rate, differs from what would be set by the market if the currency were allowed to float. By this reasoning, governments that take policy actions to sustain an exchange rate peg, such as intervening in currency markets, most likely have misaligned currencies. Additionally, this view suggests that floating currencies, by definition, cannot be misaligned, since their values are determined by market forces.

For other economists, a currency can be misaligned even if it is a floating rate. This is the case if the exchange rate differs from its long-term equilibrium value, which is based on economic fundamentals and eliminates short-term factors that can cause the exchange rate to fluctuate. Defining or estimating an equilibrium exchange rate is not a straightforward process and is complex. Economists disagree on the factors that determine an equilibrium exchange rate, and whether the concept is a valid one, particularly when applied to countries with floating exchange rates. Economists have developed a number of models for calculating differences between actual exchange rates and equilibrium exchange rates. Estimates of whether a currency is misaligned, and if so, by how much, can vary widely depending on the model used.[19]

## GENERAL DEBATES OVER "CURRENCY WARS"

Amid heightened concerns about slow growth and high unemployment in many countries, disagreements over exchange rate policies have broadened after the global financial crisis. In 2010, Brazil's finance minister, Guido Mantega, declared that a "currency war" had broken out in the global economy.[20]

At the heart of current disagreements is whether or not countries are using policies to intentionally push down the value of their currency in order to gain a trade advantage at the expense of other countries. A weak currency makes exports cheaper to foreigners and imports more expensive to domestic consumers. This can lead to higher production of exports and import-competing goods, which could help spur export-led growth and job creation in the export sector.

However, if one country weakens its currency, there can be negative implications for certain sectors in other countries. In general, a weaker currency in one country can hurt exporters in other countries, since their exports become relatively more expensive and may fall as a result. Additionally, domestic firms producing import-competing goods may find it harder to compete with imports from countries with weak currencies, since weak currencies lower the cost of imports. Under certain circumstances, policies used to drive down the value of a currency in one country can cause other countries to run persistent trade deficits (imports exceed exports) that can be difficult to adjust and can be associated with the build-up of debt.

For these reasons, some economists view efforts to boost exports through a weaker exchange rate as "unfair" to other countries and a type of "beggar-thy-neighbor" policy—the benefit the country gets from the policy comes at the expense of other countries. These views are particularly rooted in the experience in the 1930s, during which, some economists argue, countries devalued their currencies to boost exports, in response to widespread high unemployment and negative economic conditions.[21] The devaluations in the 1930s are referred to as "competitive devaluations," since a devaluation in one country was often offset by a devaluation in another country, making it difficult for any country to gain a lasting advantage.[22] Some economists view the competitive devaluations of the 1930s as detrimental to international trade, and, in addition to protectionist trade policies, as exacerbating the Great Depression.

Many economists disagree that "currency wars" and competitive devaluations are currently underway in the global economy and argue that, if they are, they are not necessarily bad for the global economy. Because currency devaluations can often involve printing domestic currency, or implementing expansionary monetary policies, they can stimulate short-term economic growth.[23] If enough countries engage in currency interventions, then there may be no net change in relative exchange rate levels and the simultaneous currency interventions may help reflate the global economy and boost global economic growth. Economists of this viewpoint argue that competitive devaluations of the 1930s did not cause the Great Depression and, in fact, actually helped end it.[24]

Additionally, a weak currency in one country does not have an unambiguous negative effect on other countries. Instead, consumers and certain sectors may benefit when other countries have weak currencies. In particular, consumers that purchase imports from abroad benefit when other countries have weak currencies, because imports become cheaper. Additionally, businesses that rely on inputs from overseas also benefit when other countries have weak currencies, by lowering the costs of inputs and thus the overall cost of production.

## SPECIFIC DEBATES OVER EXCHANGE RATES

In current debates about exchange rates and whether countries are engaged in unfair currency policies to weaken their currencies, two major types of concerns have been raised: first, concerns about countries engaged in interventions in foreign currency markets, and second, concerns about the effects of expansionary monetary policies in some developed countries on exchange rate levels.

### Currency Interventions

Governments have various mechanisms they can use to weaken, or devalue, their currency, or sustain a lower exchange rate than would exist in the absence of government intervention. One way is intervening in foreign exchange markets or, more specifically, selling domestic currency in exchange for foreign currency. These interventions increase the supply of domestic currency relative to other currencies in foreign exchange markets, pushing the price of the currency down. The foreign currency is typically then invested in foreign assets, most commonly government bonds.

Concerns about currency interventions are not new. For nearly a decade, various policy makers and analysts have raised concerns about China's interventions in foreign exchange markets to maintain, in their view, an undervalued currency relative to the U.S. dollar. Since the global financial crisis, however, concerns about currency interventions have become more widespread, as more countries, including Switzerland and others, have intervened in foreign exchange markets, in the view of some analysts, to lower the value of their currency.[25]

## China[26]

Over the past decade, the Chinese government has tightly managed the value of its currency, the renminbi (RMB) or yuan, against the U.S. dollar.[27] Some policy makers and analysts believe that China's currency policies keep the RMB undervalued relative to the U.S. dollar. They argue that China's policies give Chinese exports an "unfair" trade advantage against U.S. exports and are a major contributing factor to the U.S. trade deficit with China.

In 1994, China began to peg its currency to the U.S. dollar and kept it pegged to the U.S. dollar at a constant rate through 2005. In July 2005, it moved to a managed peg system, in which the government allowed the currency to fluctuate within a range, and the currency began to appreciate. In 2008, China halted appreciation of the RMB, due to concerns about the effects of the global financial crisis on Chinese exports. In 2012, China again allowed more flexibility in the value of the RMB against the U.S. dollar. Between 2005 and the end of 2012, the RMB appreciated by almost 25% against the dollar (**Figure 2**).[28]

The Chinese government has used various policies, including intervening in foreign currency markets and capital controls, to manage this appreciation of the RMB against the U.S. dollar. It does so primarily by printing yuan and selling it for U.S. currency and assets denominated in U.S. dollars, usually U.S. government bonds. It also manages the value of its exchange rate through capital controls that limit buying and selling of RMB.[29] As China has engaged in currency interventions, its holdings of foreign exchange reserves have increased, from $715 billion in the first quarter of 2005 to $3,463 billion in the first quarter of 2013 (**Figure 2**), equivalent to about 38% of China's GDP.[30] Some economists view the sustained, substantial increase in foreign exchange reserves as evidence that the Chinese government keeps the value of the RMB below what it would be if the RMB were allowed to float freely.

More recently, some economists are starting to question whether the yuan is still undervalued against the U.S. dollar when adjusting for differences in price levels (the real exchange rate), and if so, by how much, particularly as inflation has increased in China.[31] They point to the fact that foreign exchange reserves have not grown as quickly since 2011 as some evidence of this adjustment. In July 2012, the IMF changed its assessment of the RMB's value from significantly undervalued to moderately undervalued.[32]

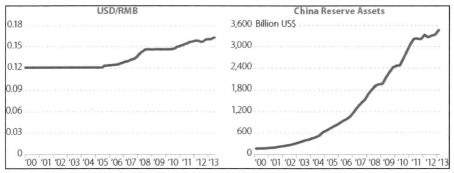

Source: Federal Reserve; IMF, International Financial Statistics.

Note: For the graph on the left, an increase represents an appreciation of the RMB relative to the U.S. dollar.

Figure 2. China's Exchange Rate and Foreign Exchange Reserves.

### Switzerland

Before the global financial crisis of 2008-2009, Switzerland had a floating exchange rate. During the crisis, the Swiss franc was viewed as a "safe haven" currency, or a currency that investors trusted more than others and would therefore buy in times of uncertainty.[33] Increased investor demand for the Swiss franc put upward pressure on the currency, which, in turn, raised concerns for the Swiss government about the competitiveness of Swiss exports. In 2009 and 2010, the Swiss central bank (the National Bank of Switzerland) intervened in foreign exchange markets to prevent or limit appreciation of the Swiss franc against the euro, by selling Swiss francs for foreign currencies.[34] When a worsening of the Eurozone crisis put additional upward pressure on the Swiss franc, the Swiss central bank announced in September 2011 that it would buy "unlimited quantities" of foreign currency to keep the Swiss franc from appreciating above a specific value (**Figure 3**).[35]

As a result of its currency interventions, Switzerland's foreign exchange reserves increased more than tenfold, from $46 billion in the fourth quarter of 2008 to $470 billion in the first quarter of 2013 (**Figure 3**), about 73% of Swiss GDP.[36] Before the financial crisis, the Swiss central bank had last intervened in the foreign exchange market in 1995.[37]

Many economists argue that the recent interventions by the Swiss central bank have held the value of the Swiss franc lower than it would be otherwise (if the currency floated freely and the Swiss central bank did not intervene in foreign exchange markets). They argue that this has given Swiss exports an advantage, helping Switzerland maintain a trade surplus and one of the lowest unemployment rates in Europe.[38] However, some economists have noted that Switzerland's trading partners have generally not "kicked up much fuss" over its interventions, and that Switzerland's interventions are the "overlooked" currency war in Europe.[39] This could be due to the small size of the Swiss economy, and a perception held by some that Swiss interventions are a defensive measure against developments in the rest of Europe that are beyond its control.

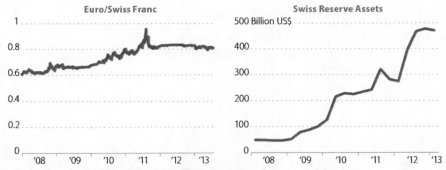

Source: European Central Bank; IMF, *International Financial Statistics*.
Note: For the graph on the left, an increase represents an appreciation of the Swiss
     franc relative to the euro.

Figure 3. Switzerland's Exchange Rate and Foreign Exchange Reserves.

### Other Countries

Other examples of interventions to weaken currencies since the global financial crisis include, among others:

- **Japan**, which sold yen in foreign exchange markets in 2010 and 2011. Japan's interventions in March 2011 were unusual in that they were supported with corresponding interventions by the other G-7 countries to weaken the yen. A crisis in Japan (earthquake, tsunami, and threat of nuclear crisis) in March 2011 had sparked a sharp appreciation of the yen, which some feared would throw the world's third-largest economy back into recession, prompting the coordinated interventions;[40]

- **South Korea**, which is believed to have intervened in currency markets intermittently to hold down the value of the won in the latter part of 2012 and early 2013;[41] and
- **New Zealand**, whose central bank revealed in May 2013 that it had intervened in currency markets to stem appreciation of its currency, the New Zealand dollar (nicknamed the kiwi).[42]

More generally, according to a December 2012 study by the Peterson Institute of International Economics (PIIE), more than 20 countries have cumulatively increased their foreign exchange reserves by nearly $1 trillion annually for several years, mainly through interventions in foreign currency markets, and as a result have been able to keep their currencies "substantially undervalued."[43] The study identifies China, Denmark, Hong Kong, South Korea, Malaysia, Singapore, Switzerland, and Taiwan as most heavily engaged in currency interventions.

### *Debates*

A number of countries are actively intervening, or have recently intervened, in foreign exchange markets to lower the value of their currencies, and there are different views among economists about the consequences of these interventions for other countries. Some economists argue that currency interventions have helped countries give their exports a boost at the expense of other countries. The December 2012 study by the PIIE estimates that currency interventions have caused the U.S. trade deficit to increase by $200 billion to $500 billion per year and the U.S. economy to lose between 1 million and 5 million jobs.[44] The study also argues that currency interventions have adversely affected the economies of Australia, Brazil, Canada, the Eurozone, India, and Mexico, in addition to a number of other developing economies.

Other economists are skeptical that one country's interventions in foreign exchange markets have had adverse consequences for other countries. For example, some economists argue that interventions in foreign exchange markets by other countries change the composition of output in the United States (particularly the size of the export and domestic-oriented sectors), but do not reduce the overall employment or output levels in the U.S. economy. Some economists also question whether currency interventions have long-lasting effects on exchange rate levels, particularly for countries with floating currencies. They argue that the large size of international capital flows overwhelms, in the long term, government purchases and sales of foreign currencies, and that other economic fundamentals, such as interest rates, inflation rates, and overall economic performance, have much greater effects on exchange rate levels.

Still other economists argue that it is hard to make generalizations about the effects of currency interventions, and that, depending on the specific circumstances, currency interventions may or may not be "fair" policies.[45] For example, they argue that relevant factors can include:

- Does the government intervene in currency markets to sometimes strengthen and sometimes weaken its currency, or does it always intervene to weaken its currency? "Two-way" interventions (sometimes strengthening the currency, sometimes weakening the currency) may be evidence that the country is using currency interventions to sustain a pegged exchange rate that is close to its longterm fundamental or equilibrium value. Some economists argue that "one-way" interventions (always selling domestic currency) may be evidence that the government is using interventions to sustain a currency that is below the currency's fundamental or equilibrium value.

- Does the government intervene periodically, or on a continual basis? Periodic interventions may smooth potentially disruptive short-term fluctuations in the exchange rate and help the country build foreign exchange reserves, which can help it guard against economic crises. Sustained, or long-term, interventions may create negative distortions in the global economy.

- Does the government allow the intervention to increase its domestic money supply, or does the government "sterilize" the intervention to prevent an increase in its domestic money supply? When some governments intervene in currency markets by selling domestic currency, they allow the domestic money supply to increase. This is called an unsterilized intervention. When other countries (such as China and, sometimes, Switzerland) intervene, they do not allow their money supply to increase. Instead, when they sell domestic currency in exchange for foreign currency, they then sell a corresponding quantity of domestic government bonds to remove the extra domestic currency from circulation. This is called a sterilized intervention. It may matter to other countries whether the intervening country sterilizes the intervention or not. For example, increasing the money supply may help increase domestic demand, which in certain circumstances can cause consumers to buy more, not fewer, imports from other countries. Additionally, an increase in the money supply may cause prices to rise in the medium term. This may mean that the exchange rate adjusted for inflation (the real exchange rate) may not change in the medium term (after prices adjust), even if the nominal exchange rate (the exchange rate not adjusted for inflation) falls.

## Expansionary Monetary Policies

In addition to intervening directly in foreign exchange markets, governments can weaken the value of their currency through expansionary monetary policies. Monetary policy is the process by which a government (usually the central bank) controls the supply of money in an economy, such as by changing the interest rates through buying and selling government bonds. Changes in the money supply can impact the value of the currency. For example, increasing the supply of British pounds can cause the price of the pound to fall.

Some emerging markets, particularly Brazil, have been critical of the expansionary monetary policies adopted by the United States, the United Kingdom, and the Eurozone in response to the global financial crisis of 2008-2009. A number of countries have also raised concerns about Japan's monetary policies, following a major policy shift in late 2012 and early 2013.

### Quantitative Easing in the United States, UK, and Eurozone[46]

The United States, the United Kingdom, and, to a lesser extent, the Eurozone adopted expansionary monetary policies to respond to the economic recession following the global financial crisis of 2008-2009. In addition to cutting interest rates, the Federal Reserve, the Bank of England, and the European Central Bank (ECB) used quantitative easing to provide further monetary stimulus. Quantitative easing is an unconventional form of monetary policy that expands the money supply through government purchases of assets, usually government bonds. Quantitative easing is typically used when more conventional monetary policy tools are no longer feasible, for example, when short-term interest rates cannot be cut because they are already near zero.

Some emerging markets have argued that because the U.S. dollar, the British pound, and the euro are floating currencies, expansionary policies in these countries have caused these currencies to depreciate against the currencies of emerging markets. For example, Brazil has argued that quantitative easing in developed countries was a key factor in causing its currency (the real) to appreciate by more than 25% against the dollar between the start of 2009 and the end of the third quarter of 2010 (see **Figure 4**), when Brazil's finance minister, Guido Mantega, declared that a currency "war" had broken out in the global economy.[47] Brazil imposed some short-term controls on inflows of capital into Brazil (capital controls) to stem appreciation of the real.[48]

In response to the concerns of emerging markets, many policy makers and analysts have argued that the Federal Reserve, the Bank of England, and the ECB adopted expansionary monetary policies for domestic purposes (combatting the recession), and that any effect on their currencies was a side-effect or by-product of the policy.[49] For example, during a Senate Banking Committee hearing in February 2013, the Chairman of the Federal Reserve, Ben Bernanke, stressed that the Federal Reserve is not engaged in a currency war or targeting the value of the U.S. dollar.[50]

Instead, he emphasized that monetary policy is being used to achieve domestic economic objectives (high employment and price stability). He also stressed that monetary policies to strengthen aggregate demand in the United States are not "zero-sum," because they raise the demand for the exports of other countries.

The concerns of emerging markets about the effects of quantitative easing have eased in recent months. As developed countries have started discussing rolling back expansionary monetary policies, the real has weakened substantially against the U.S. dollar (see **Figure 4**). Brazil's government, in fact, has started expressing concerns about the real becoming too weak, and in August 2013, intervened in foreign currency markets to strengthen its currency.[51] The concerns of emerging-market economies about the potential rollback of quantitative easing policies in developed countries, including the United States, were a major topic of discussion at the September 2013 G-20 summit in St. Petersburg, Russia.[52]

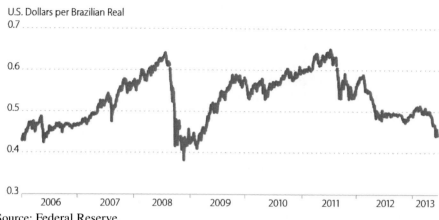

Source: Federal Reserve.

Note: An increase represents an appreciation of the Brazilian real relative to the U.S. dollar.

Figure 4. U.S. Dollar-Brazilian Real Exchange Rate.

### Japan and "Abenomics"

Concerns have also been recently raised about major changes in Japan's monetary policy and their effects on the value of the yen. Elected in December 2012, Prime Minister Shinzo Abe has made it a priority of his administration to grow Japan's economy and eliminate deflation (falling prices), which has plagued Japan for many years. His economic plan, nicknamed "Abenomics," relies on three major economic policies: expansionary monetary policies, fiscal stimulus, and structural reforms. To promote expansionary monetary policy, Japan's central bank (the Bank of Japan) unveiled a host of new measures in the first half of 2013, including goals to double the monetary base (commercial bank reserves plus currency circulating in the public) and to double its holdings of Japanese government bonds. By buying government bonds in exchange for yen, the Bank of Japan can increase Japan's money supply.

Changes in Japan's monetary policies, along with fiscal stimulus measures, appear to be contributing to a strengthening of Japan's economy. For example, in July 2013, the IMF upgraded its forecast of growth in Japan for 2013, from 1.5% to 2.0%.[53] However, the expansionary monetary policies may have also contributed to a relatively sharp depreciation of the yen, which fell more than 25% between mid-2012 and mid-2013 (see **Figure 5**), even as Japan has not directly intervened in currency markets since 2011.

Several countries have expressed their concerns about a weakening of the yen. An official from the Russian central bank reportedly warned that "Japan is weakening the yen and other countries may follow," and that "the world is on the brink of a fresh currency war."[54] Additionally, the president of China's sovereign wealth fund reportedly warned Japan against using its neighbors as a "garbage bin" by deliberately devaluing the yen, and South Korea's finance minister argued that Japan's weakening yen hurts his country's economy more than threats from North Korea.[55] Movements in Japan's currency have also created concerns for some Members of Congress, with concerns being raised about the currency policies in the context of the TPP, where Japan is one of the negotiating parties.

Others argue that a weakening yen in recent months has partially offset the slow, but continued, appreciation of the yen in the preceding several years (**Figure 5**). For example, in January 2012, the IMF estimated that the Japanese yen was "moderately overvalued from a medium-term perspective."[56] Some also argue that, rather than targeting the value of the currency, Japan's monetary policies are targeting domestic objectives, namely, beating deflation that has plagued the economy for many years. Japan's finance minister, Taro Aso, reportedly stated that "monetary easing is aimed at pulling Japan out of deflation quickly. It is not accurate at all to criticize (us) for manipulating currencies."[57]

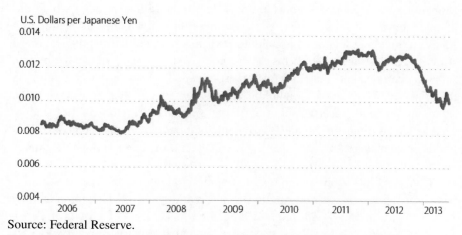

Source: Federal Reserve.
Note: A decrease represents a depreciation of the yen relative to the U.S. dollar.

Figure 5. U.S. Dollar-Japanese Yen Exchange Rate.

## *Debates*

There is debate over whether the expansionary monetary policies, including quantitative easing, implemented by some developed economies have been "beggar-thy-neighbor" policies. Some argue that expansionary monetary policies have unfairly caused the currencies of developed countries to depreciate against other countries, giving the exports of developed countries an "unfair" export boost. However, most economists agree that the expansionary policies in the United States, the UK, the Eurozone, and Japan have been designed to stimulate their domestic economies and will, in the medium term, cause prices to rise. As a result, they argue that there will be little effect on the real exchange rate (the exchange rate adjusted for differences in prices across countries) in the medium term (as prices increase), even if the nominal exchange rate (the exchange rate not adjusted for differences in prices across countries) falls in the short term. However, it should be noted that inflation in all these countries remains very low, to date.

Additionally, some argue that the expansionary policies stimulate domestic consumption and investment, which ordinarily leads to higher, not lower, imports from other countries, all else being equal.[58] They argue that the net effect of quantitative easing and similar policies on trading partners is not necessarily negative and could be positive in some instances. For example, the IMF estimated that the first round of quantitative easing in the United States resulted in substantial output gains for the rest of the world, and that the second round generated modest output gains for the rest of the world.[59]

For some economists, then, a key question to evaluate whether expansionary monetary policies are "fair" or "unfair" in the context of claims about "currency wars" is:

- Is it appropriate for countries to adopt expansionary monetary policies to combat a domestic economic recession, even if some sectors in other countries may be adversely affected in the short run?: Some economists argue that it is entirely "natural" for countries to unilaterally adopt the monetary policies to suit their specific needs of the domestic economy, and that countries should use expansionary monetary policies to respond to economic recessions.[60] Moreover, most central banks, including the Fed, are pursuing statutory mandates that do not include foreign exchange rate requirements and responsibilities. Other economists argue that countries have a number of policy tools to respond to economic recessions, not just monetary policy, and that in today's globalized economy, a country should consider the potential negative spillover effects on other countries in its decision-making process.

# ADDRESSING DISAGREEMENTS OVER EXCHANGE RATES

Government policies that impact exchange rates have been a source of contention among countries. Various avenues have been developed or explored over the years to address specific currency disputes, both at the multilateral level and through U.S. law, with varying degrees of impact.

On the multilateral front, countries have made commitments to refrain from "manipulating" their exchange rates to gain an unfair trade advantage through the International Monetary Fund (IMF). Additionally, some argue that commitments made in the context of the World Trade Organization (WTO) are relevant to disagreements over exchange rates, although this view is disputed. Exchange rate issues have also been addressed in the past through less formal channels of international economic coordination among small groups of developed economies.

In addition to these multilateral forums, the United States has also adopted legislation to address unfair exchange rate policies pursued by other countries. In 1988, Congress enacted legislation to address "currency manipulation" by other countries. Congress has also included provisions on exchange rates in previous TPA legislation.

Exchange rate issues have been a key source of discussion at recent G-7 and G-20 meetings, but little formal or concrete action has occurred beyond these discussions.[61] Neither the IMF nor the U.S. Treasury Department has found any country to be manipulating its exchange rate in recent years.

## Forums to Potentially Address Disagreements

### *International Monetary Fund*

With a nearly universal membership of 188 countries, the IMF is focused on promoting international monetary stability.[62] The IMF has engaged on the exchange rate policies of its member countries as part of its mandate, arguably motivated by the experience of competitive devaluations in the 1930s.[63] Its role on exchange rates has evolved over time.[64] Currently, IMF member countries have agreed to several obligations on exchange rates in the IMF's Articles of Agreement, the document that lays out the rules governing the IMF and establishes a "code of conduct" for IMF member countries.[65] The Articles state that countries can use whatever exchange rate system they wish—fixed or floating—so long as they follow certain guidelines; that countries should seek, in their foreign exchange and monetary policies, to promote orderly economic growth and financial stability; and that the IMF should engage in "firm" surveillance over the exchange rate policies of its members.[66]

The Articles also state that IMF member countries are to "avoid manipulating exchange rates or the international monetary system in order to prevent effective balance of payments adjustment or to gain an unfair advantage over other members."[67] An IMF Decision, issued in 1977 and updated in 2007 and 2012, provides further guidance that, among other things, "a member will only be considered to be manipulating exchange rates in order to gain an unfair competitive advantage over other members if the Fund determines both that: (a) the member is engaged in these policies for the purposes of securing fundamental exchange rate misalignment in the form of an undervalued exchange rate; and (b) the purpose of securing such misalignment is to increase net exports."[68]

If a member country were to be found to be in violation of its obligations to the IMF, under the rules laid out in the Articles, it could be punished through restrictions on its access to IMF funding, suspension of its voting rights at the IMF, or, ultimately, expulsion from the IMF.[69]

To date, the IMF has never publicly labeled a member country a currency manipulator.[70] Some argue that the IMF's definition of currency "manipulation" has made it tough to go after currency "manipulators." They argue that it requires the IMF to determine or demonstrate that policies shaping the exchange rate level have been for the express purpose of increasing net exports, and that "intent" is hard to establish.[71] Even if the IMF could demonstrate a country is manipulating its exchange rate under its definition of the term, some analysts also argue that, in practice, the IMF does not have a credible mechanism for dealing with "manipulators," particularly countries that are not reliant on IMF financing.[72] They argue that it is extremely unlikely the IMF would actually strip violators of their IMF voting rights or expel them from the institution.

### World Trade Organization

With 159 member countries, the WTO is the principal international organization governing world trade. It was established in 1995 as a successor institution to the General Agreement on Tariffs and Trade (GATT), a post-World War II institution intended to liberalize and promote nondiscrimination in trade among countries. Unique among the major international trade and finance organizations, the WTO has a mechanism for enforcing its rules through a dispute settlement process.

Given the relationship between exchange rates and trade, some have argued that the World Trade Organization (WTO) has a role to play in responding to currency disputes. Some analysts and lawyers have examined whether WTO provisions allow for recourse against countries that are unfairly undervaluing its currency.[73]

One aspect of the debate is whether WTO agreement on export subsidies applies to countries with undervalued currencies. The WTO Agreement on Subsidies and Countervailing Measures specifies that countries may not provide subsidies to help promote their national exports, and countries are entitled to levy countervailing duties on imported products that receive subsidies from their national government.[74] Some economists maintain that an undervalued currency lowers a firm's cost of production relative to world prices and therefore helps encourage exports. Some argue, then, that an undervalued currency should count as an export subsidy. It is not clear, however, whether intentional undervaluation of a country's currency is an export subsidy under the WTO's specific definition of the term, and thus is eligible for recourse through countervailing duties under WTO agreements. For example, the subsidy must be, among other things, specific to an industry and not provided generally to all producers. There is debate over whether intentional undervaluation of a currency is "industry specific" because it applies to everyone.

Another aspect of the debate relates to a provision in the GATT (the WTO agreement on international trade in goods), which states that member countries "shall not, by exchange action, frustrate intent of the provisions" of the agreement.[75] Some analysts argue that policies to undervalue a currency are protectionist policies, and thus should count as an exchange rate action that frustrates the intent of the GATT. Others argue that the language is too vague to apply to undervalued currencies.[76] Specifically, they argue that the language was written to apply to an international system of exchange rates that no longer exists (the system of fixed exchange rates, combined with capital controls, that prevailed from the end of World War II to the early 1970s).

No dispute over exchange rates has been brought before the WTO,[77] and whether currency disputes fall under the WTO's jurisdiction remains a contested issue.[78]

### *Less Formal Multilateral Coordination: The G-7 and the G-20*

In addition to formal international institutions focused on economic issues, like the IMF and the WTO, countries also use less formal forums to coordinate economic policies. Before the global financial crisis of 2008-2009, the primary forum was a small group of seven advanced economies, the G-7.[79] Following the crisis, the G-20, a larger group of advanced and emerging-market countries, became the premier forum for international economic coordination.[80]

In the past, small groups of advanced economies had had more success in addressing currency issues through this type of less formal international cooperation. For example, in 1985, France, West Germany, Japan, the United States, and the UK signed the Plaza Accord, in which countries agreed to intervene in currency markets to depreciate the U.S. dollar in relation to the Japanese yen and the German deutsche mark to address the U.S. trade deficit. In 1987, six countries (the five signatories of the Plaza Accord, plus Canada) signed the Louvre Accord, in which they agreed to halt the depreciation of the U.S. dollar through a host of different policy measures, including taxes, public spending, and interest rates. Some economists argue that the Plaza and Louvre Accords were successful because they reinforced economic fundamentals that were pushing exchange rates in the desired direction.

Additionally, small groups of countries have executed coordinated interventions in foreign exchange markets to shape the relative value of currencies. For example, the G-7 countries have coordinated interventions a number of times: in 1995, to halt the dollar's fall against the yen; in 2000, to support the value of the euro after its introduction; and in 2011, to stem appreciation of the yen following a major crisis in Japan.[81] This coordination has occurred on an ad hoc, voluntary basis. It is not based on any specific set of rules or commitments on exchange rates, and has been limited to a small group of advanced economies.

### *U.S. Law: The 1988 Trade Act*

In 1988, Congress enacted the "Exchange Rates and International Economic Policy Coordination Act of 1988" as part of the Omnibus Trade and Competitiveness Act of 1988 (the 1988 Trade Act),[82] when many policy makers were concerned about the appreciation of the U.S. dollar and large U.S. trade deficits.[83] A key component of this act requires the Treasury Department to analyze on an annual basis the exchange rate policies of foreign countries, in consultation with the IMF, and "consider whether countries manipulate the rate of exchange between their currency and the United States dollar for purposes of preventing effective balance of payments adjustments or gaining unfair competitive advantage in international trade." If "manipulation" is occurring with respect to countries that have (1) global currency account surpluses and (2) significant bilateral trade surpluses with the United States, the Secretary of the Treasury is to initiate negotiations, through the IMF or bilaterally, to ensure adjustment in the exchange rate and eliminate the "unfair" trade advantage. The Secretary of the Treasury is not required to start negotiations in cases where they would have a serious detrimental impact on vital U.S. economic and security interests.

Additionally, the act requires the Treasury Secretary to submit a report annually to the Senate and House Banking Committees, on or before October 15, with written six-month updates (on April 15), and the Secretary is expected to testify on the reports as requested.[84] The reports are to address a host of issues related to exchange rate policies, such as currency market developments; currency interventions undertaken to adjust the exchange rate of the dollar; the impact of the exchange rate on U.S. competitiveness; and the outcomes of Treasury negotiations on currency issues, among others.

Since the 1988 Trade Act was enacted, the Treasury Department has identified three countries as manipulating their currencies under the Trade Act's terms: China, Taiwan, and South Korea.[85]

These designations occurred in the late 1980s and early 1990s; Treasury has not found currency manipulation under the terms of the 1988 Trade Act since it last cited China in 1994. Some Members of Congress have been concerned by what they perceive as inaction by the Treasury Department on currency manipulation. In 2004, Congress passed legislation asking the Treasury Secretary to submit a report "describing how statutory provisions addressing currency manipulation by America's trading partners ... can be better clarified administratively to provide for improved and more predictable evaluation, and to enable the problem of currency manipulation to be better understood by the American people."[86] In 2005, the Government Accountability Office (GAO) completed a study on Treasury's assessments of whether countries manipulate their currencies for trade advantage.[87] One conclusion in the report was that "Treasury has generally complied with the reporting requirements for its exchange rate reports, although its discussion of U.S. economic impacts has become less specific over time."

### Trade Promotion Authority and Trade Agreements

Given the potential links between exchange rate policies of other countries and the competitiveness of U.S. industry and exports, Congress has referenced addressing currency issues in previous TPA authorizations. For example, in the Omnibus Trade and Competitiveness Act of 1988, which granted "fast track" authority (the precursor to TPA) to the President, the President was required, among other things, to submit a report to Congress with supporting information after entering a trade agreement. One part of this report was "describing the efforts made by the President to obtain international exchange rate equilibrium."[88]

Additionally, when TPA was last renewed in 2002, Congress included exchange rate issues as a priority that the Administration should promote. The legislation stipulated that the Administration should "seek to establish consultative mechanisms among parties to trade agreements to examine the trade consequences of significant and unanticipated currency movements and to scrutinize whether a foreign government engaged in a pattern of manipulating its currency to promote a competitive advantage in international trade."[89]

A number of free trade agreements (FTAs) were negotiated under the 2002 version of TPA, with Congress approving implementing legislation for FTAs with Chile, Singapore, Australia, Morocco, the Dominican Republic and the Central American countries (CAFTA-DR), Bahrain, Oman, Peru, Colombia, Panama, and South Korea. It is not clear to what extent currency issues were salient issues in the negotiations or in the final agreements.

## Responses to Current Disagreements

To the extent that there has been a formal multilateral response to current disagreements over exchange rates, it has been through discussions at G-7 and G-20 meetings. During meetings in February 2013, for example, the G-7 nations reaffirmed their "long-standing commitment to market-determined exchange rates" and to "not target exchange rates."[90] The G-20 countries pledged to "refrain from competitive devaluation" in February 2013,[91] and more recently in September 2013, that central banks "have committed that future changes to monetary policy settings will continue to be carefully calibrated and clearly communicated."[92] G-7 and G-20 commitments are non-binding, although other enforcement mechanisms, including peer pressure, have been used to ensure compliance in the past.

Current disagreements over exchange rates have not resulted in the IMF or the Treasury Department labeling any countries as currency manipulators, and no country has filed a dispute over exchange rate policies at the WTO. Starting in 2011, Brazil did present three papers on exchange rates and the role of the WTO for discussion at the WTO Working Group on Trade, Debt, and Finance. Reportedly, many other WTO members have approached the discussions with "reserve and skepticism" and believed that the IMF would be the appropriate forum for such a discussion.[93]

Some analysts and policy makers have been concerned that current disagreements have not resulted in more formal action, particularly by the IMF and the Treasury Department, which have the clearest rules pertaining to currency manipulation. They argue that currency manipulation has occurred, but the current frameworks are ineffective at dealing with it. For example, they argue that it is hard to demonstrate that exchange rate policies have been for the express purpose of increasing net exports; the IMF does not have a clear enforcement mechanism for its rules on exchange rates; and the Treasury Department fears retaliation from countries it unilaterally labels as "manipulators." One policy expert has stated that the greatest flaw in the international financial architecture is its failure to effectively counter and deter competitive currency policies.[94]

Other analysts and policy makers contend that the current frameworks on "currency manipulation" are effective. They argue that formal action by the IMF and the Treasury Department has not occurred because countries have not engaged in policies that violate international commitments on exchange rates or triggered U.S. laws pertaining to currency manipulation. Some analysts also believe that the Treasury Department has at various times urged countries to address exchange rate issues behind-the-scenes, even if it has not publicly labeled any countries as currency manipulators in recent years.[95]

# POLICY OPTIONS FOR CONGRESS

Some Members of Congress have proposed taking action on currency issues, because they are concerned about the impact of other countries' exchange rate policies on the competitiveness of U.S. exports and import-competing firms. Some Members could also be concerned that other countries have accused the United States of engaging in "currency wars." If Members did decide to take action on exchange rates, there are a number of options for doing so, some of which Members are already pursuing. Policy options could include, among others:

**(1) Maintaining the status quo:** Even though Members may be concerned about supporting U.S. exports and jobs from "unfair" exchange rate policies adopted by other countries, there may be a number of reasons to refrain from taking action on exchange rate disputes:

- There is much debate among economists on how to calculate a currency's "equilibrium" or "fundamental" long-term value, making the classification of currencies as undervalued or overvalued complex and subject to much discussion, with different models at times yielding very different results. Some economists also believe that currency interventions have limited, short-term effects, particularly on floating currencies, given the high volumes of capital flows.
- U.S. imports from trading partners with weak currencies are less expensive than they would be otherwise. Lower-cost imports may benefit U.S. businesses that purchase inputs from abroad and U.S. consumers.
- Unilaterally labeling a country as a currency manipulator or leading a multilateral charge against currency manipulation could trigger retaliation by other countries. For example, the United States has a low savings rate and benefits from low interest rates. Countries labeled as currency "manipulators" could buy fewer U.S. government bonds, making it more expensive and potentially harder for the U.S. government to finance its budget deficit.
- Tensions over exchange rates could dissipate as the global economy strengthens, particularly if developed economies end quantitative easing. For example, Brazil's concerns about the real appreciating against the U.S. dollar have reversed in recent months (and now Brazil is concerned about the real depreciating against the U.S. dollar too much).

**(2) Urging the Administration to address currency disputes at the IMF or WTO:** Addressing currency disputes in formal international institutions may provide broad, multilateral support for decisions that are reached. The IMF and the WTO have been the international institutions identified as best suited for dealing with exchange rate disputes, because the IMF has the clearest set of commitments relating to currency manipulation, and the WTO is unique among international financial institutions in that it has a clear enforcement mechanism. However, addressing disputes over exchange rates at the IMF and WTO may run into obstacles. For example, the IMF Executive Board may find it too politically sensitive to label a country as a "currency manipulator." Congress could ask the Administration to push for changes to IMF and/or WTO rules to allow currency disputes to be addressed more clearly under these organizations, but this could be a complicated process that requires multilateral consensus.

**(3) Urging the Administration to strengthen informal international cooperation on exchange rates:** For example, Congress could urge the Treasury Department to continue its push for G-20 commitments on (1) greater transparency of foreign reserve data and currency intervention operations; and (2) avoidance of official public statements intended to influence exchange rate levels.[96] Additionally, Congress could also urge the Administration to push for informal agreements to re-align the value of currencies, similar to the Plaza Accord and the Louvre Accord in the 1980s. However, some question whether informal cooperation can effectively foster cooperation on exchange rates consistently, not just on an as-needed or ad-hoc basis. The G-7 excludes large emerging market economies that are major players in the global economy, but, at the same time, the G-20 may be too large and heterogeneous to reach meaningful agreements. Also, since agreements reached at the G-7 and G-20 are non-binding, questions have been raised about the effectiveness of these forums. This approach would also be unlikely to address manipulation by countries outside the G-7 or G-20, although some argue that G-20 action in particular would involve the major economies in the international economy.

**(4) Addressing currency issues in trade agreements or as a negotiating objective in TPA:** Congress could address concerns about the exchange rate policies of other countries by urging the Administration to address currency issues in the free trade agreements currently under negotiation, including the TPP and TTIP. For example, Representative Levin released a proposal to address currency manipulation in the TPP in July 2013.[97] With regards to any legislation renewing TPA, Congress could also identify currency issues as a trade policy priority, similar to the provisions included in the 2002 TPA legislation, or include currency issues as a more formal trade negotiating objective.

Seeking to include currency issues in a trade agreement could make the agreement more difficult to conclude. There are also different views about how currency issues could or should be addressed. Some have called for enforceable provisions, but there may be disagreement over how exchange rate disputes would be adjudicated. Others have called for cooperative frameworks to examine currency issues. Additionally, any negotiated agreement on currency disagreements would be limited in scope, because it would apply to negotiating parties to the agreement and not to countries in the global economy more broadly.

**(5) Passing new legislation on undervalued exchange rates or amending existing legislation on currency manipulation:** Some argue that legislation could directly address the concerns of certain U.S. exporters and import-sensitive producers about "unfair" exchange rate policies of other countries, and could provide U.S. exporters with recourse and/or encourage other countries to push up the value of their currencies. Additionally, a possible advantage of legislation relating to countries with "undervalued" or "misaligned" currencies is that it could apply to all countries, not just a subset of countries, such as countries that are party to a trade negotiation with the United States.

Several pieces of legislation on exchange rates have been introduced in previous Congresses, and two bills have been introduced in the 113th Congress:

- **The Currency Reform for Fair Trade Act (H.R. 1276)** would affect the treatment of imports from countries with fundamentally undervalued exchange rates. If passed, it would broaden the definition of a "countervailable" subsidy (or a subsidy that could be eligible to be offset through higher import duties) to include the benefit conferred on merchandise imports into the United States from foreign countries with fundamentally undervalued currencies.[98]
- **The Currency Exchange Rate Oversight Reform Act of 2013 (S. 1114)** proposes methods for addressing exchange rate issues. Among other provisions, the legislation prescribes negotiations and consultations with countries with fundamentally misaligned exchange rates, and actions to take against "priority action" countries that have failed, or persistently failed, to take action to eliminate exchange rate misalignments.[99]

Others argue that it could be difficult to reach consensus on if, and if so, by how much, a currency is undervalued or misaligned. Additionally, if currency "manipulation" was defined in statute, it could be inflexible. As mentioned earlier, unilateral legislation could also provoke countries that are labeled as having undervalued currencies, and cause them to retaliate in ways that undermine other U.S. interests. Legislation could also harm U.S. producers and consumers that buy and use imported goods. Finally, some have raised questions about whether legislation relating to import duties would violate WTO rules.


# CONCLUSION

Exchange rates are important prices in the global economy, and changes in exchange rates have potentially substantial implications for international trade and investment flows across countries. Following the global financial crisis of 2008-2009, tensions among countries over exchange rate policies have arguably broadened. Some policy makers and analysts have expressed concerns that some governments are pursuing exchange rate policies to gain a trade advantage, as many countries grapple with economic recession or slow growth and high unemployment following the financial crisis. Concerns have focused on both government interventions in currency markets in a number of other countries, including China and Switzerland, and expansionary monetary policies in some developed economies. On the other hand, some economists argue that the effects of exchange rate policies are nuanced, creating winners and losers, and that it is hard to make generalized claims about the negative effects of "currency wars."

Members concerned about the competitiveness of the United States may want to weigh the pros and cons of taking action on exchange rate disputes. If policy makers do want to take action, a number of policy options are available. Some Members of Congress have proposed legislation to address currency undervaluation by other countries and proposed addressing currency issues in on-going trade negotiations, particularly in the context of the proposed TPP and any renewal of TPA. Members could also urge the Administration to press the issue more forcefully at international institutions, such as the IMF or WTO, or more informal forums for international cooperation, including the G-7 or the G-20.

To date, the most formal response to current tensions over exchange rates has been through discussions at G-7 and G-20 meetings. Although frameworks have been set up for addressing currency "manipulation" at the IMF and through U.S. law, neither the IMF nor the U.S. Treasury Department has taken formal action on current disputes over exchange rates. There are debates about why formal action has not been taken at these institutions. One general complicating factor in addressing currency disputes is that estimating a currency's "fundamental" or "true" value is extremely complex and subject to debate among economists.

# End Notes

[1] For example, see "Brazil Warns of World Currency War," *Reuters*, September 28, 2010; Fred Bergsten, "Currency Wars, the Economy of the United States, and Reform of the International Monetary System," Remarks at Peterson Institute for International Economics, May 16, 2013, http://www.iie.com/publications/papers/bergsten201305.pdf.

[2] For more information on TPP, see CRS Report R42694, *The Trans-Pacific Partnership Negotiations and Issues for Congress*, coordinated by Ian F. Fergusson.

[3] Representative Mike Michaud, "Majority of House Members Push Obama to Address Currency Manipulation in TPP," Press Release, June 6, 2013, http://michaud.house.gov/press-release/majority-

[4] Senator Debbie Stabenow, "Sixty Senators Urge Administration to Crack Down on Currency Manipulation in Trans-Pacific Partnership Talks," Press Release, September 24, 2013, http://www.stabenow.senate.gov/?p=press_release&id=1171. The U.S. auto industry in particular has been supportive of efforts to address currency manipulation in TPP. For example, see Michael Stumo, "American Auto Industry Applauds Senate Currency Letter," *Trade Reform*, September 25, 2013.

[5] U.S. Representative Sander Levin, "U.S.-Japan Automotive Trade: Proposal to Level the Playing Field," http://www.piie.com/publications/papers/levin20130723proposal.pdf.

[6] For example, see U.S. Congress, House Ways and Means, *U.S. Trade Representative Michael Froman*, 113th Cong., 1st sess., July 18, 2013; U.S. Congress, Senate Finance, *Confirmation Hearing on the Nomination of Michael Froman to be U.S. Trade Representative*, 113th Cong., 1st sess., June 6, 2013. For more on TTIP, see CRS Report R43158, *Proposed Transatlantic Trade and Investment Partnership (TTIP): In Brief*, by Shayerah Ilias Akhtar and Vivian C. Jones. For more information about TPA, see CRS Report RL33743, *Trade Promotion Authority (TPA) and the Role of Congress in Trade Policy*, by J. F. Hornbeck and William H. Cooper.

[7] For more on TPA, see CRS Report RL33743, *Trade Promotion Authority (TPA) and the Role of Congress in Trade Policy*, by J. F. Hornbeck and William H. Cooper.

[8] Exchange rate data in this report is from the Federal Reserve, unless otherwise noted.

[9] Bank for International Settlements, "Foreign Exchange Turnover in April 2013: Preliminary Global Results," Triennial Central Bank Survey, September 2013, https://www.bis.org/publ/rpfx13fx.pdf.

[10] For example, see "BIS Effective Exchange Rate Indices," http://www.bis.org/statistics

[11] This assumes that changes in the exchange rate are reflected in retail and consumer prices. In practice, there may be factors that limit the "pass through" of changes in the exchange rates to changes in prices. For example, contracts may lock in prices of imports and exports for a set amount of time.

[12] It may take time for changes in the exchange rate to result in changes in the volume of tradable goods and services. For example, if imports become more expensive, it may take time for domestic consumers to find suitable domestic or foreign substitutes.

[13] The Eurozone refers to the 17 European Union (EU) member states that use the euro as their currency: Austria, Belgium, Cyprus, Estonia, Finland, France, Germany, Greece, Ireland, Italy, Luxembourg, Malta, the Netherlands, Portugal, Slovakia, Spain, and Slovenia. The other 10 EU members have yet to adopt the euro or have chosen not to adopt the euro.

[14] Exchange rates were, in theory, fixed but "adjustable," meaning that countries could adjust their exchange rates to correct a "fundamental disequilibrium" in their exchange rate. In practice, it was rare for a country to adjust its exchange rate outside of a narrow band.

15  IMF, "Annual Report on Exchange Arrangements and Exchange Restrictions," 2012, http://www.imf.org/external/pubs/nft/2012/eaer/ar2012.pdf. Exchange rate data on how the exchange rate policies work in practice (the "*de facto*" exchange rate policy), which may or may not match the official description of the policy (the "*de jure*" exchange rate policy). Countries that are members of a currency union (where multiple countries may adopt use of the same currency, including the Eurozone, the East Caribbean Currency Union, the West African Economic and Monetary Union, and the Central African Economic Community) are coded according to how the currency is managed. For example, the euro is a floating currency, and individual members of the Eurozone for this purpose are counted as having adopted floating exchange rates.

16  IMF, *World Economic Outlook Database*, April 2013.

17  13% use other managed arrangements that do not fall neatly into a "soft" peg or "hard" peg category, sometimes because the government changes exchange rate policies frequently.

18  For example, see Enzo Cassino and David Oxley, "Exchange Rate Valuation and its Impact on the Real Economy," New Zealand Treasury, March 2013, http://www.rbnz.govt.nz /research_and_publications/seminars Rebecca L. Driver and Peter F. Westaway, " Concepts of Equilibrium Exchange Rates," Bank of England, Working Paper No. 248, 2004, http://www.bankofengland.co.uk /publications /Documents/workingpapers/wp248.pdf.

19  For example, see "Misleading Misalignments," *Economist*, June 21, 2007; Peter Isard, "Equilibrium Exchange Rates: Assessment Methodologies," IMF Working Paper WP/07/296, December 2007, http://www.imf.org/external/pubs/ft/wp/2007/wp07296.pdf; Treasury Department, "Semiannual Report on International Economic and Exchange Rate Policies," December 2006, Appendix 2, Exchange Rate Misalignment: What the Models Tell Us and Methodological Considerations," http://www.treasury.gov/resource-center/international/exchange-ratepolicies/Documents/2006_Appendix-2.pdf.

20  For example, see "Brazil Warns of World Currency War," *Reuters*, September 28, 2010.

21  For example, see Beth A. Simmons, *Who Adjusts? Domestic Sources of Foreign Economic Policy During the Interwar Years.* (Princeton, NJ: Princeton University Press, 1994). Not all economists characterize changes in exchange rates during the 1930s as competitive devaluations. For example, some argue that countries were forced to devalue because they were running out of gold reserves. See Douglas A. Irwin, *Trade Policy Disaster: Lessons from the 1930s* (Cambridge, MA: MIT Press, 2012).

22  Depreciation is typically used to refer to a currency weakening due to market forces. When a government undertakes specific policies to weaken the value of its currency, it is typically referred to as a devaluation.

23  For example, see Matthew O'Brien, "Currency Wars, What Are They Good For? Absolutely Ending Depressions," *The Atlantic*, February 5, 2013.

24  Barry Eichengreen, "Currency War or International Policy Coordination?," University of California, Berkeley, January 2013, http://emlab.berkeley.edu/~eichengr/curr_war_ JPM_2013.pdf.

25  For example, see Alan Beattie, "Hostilities Escalate to Hidden Currency War," *Financial Times*, September 27, 2010.

26  For more on China's currency, see CRS Report RL32165, *China's Currency: Economic Issues and Options for U.S. Trade Policy*, by Wayne M. Morrison and Marc Labonte.

27  The official name of China's currency is the renminbi (RMB), which is denominated in yuan units. Both RMB and yuan are used interchangeably to refer to China's currency.

28  Change in the nominal exchange rate (not adjusted for differences in inflation between China and the United States).

[29] The RMB is largely convertible on a current account (trade) basis, but not on a capital account basis, meaning that foreign exchange in China is not regularly obtainable for investment purposes. In other words, it can be difficult to purchase investments denominated in RMB.

[30] IMF, *International Financial Statistics*, 2013; IMF, *World Economic Outlook*, April 2013.

[31] "The Cheapest Thing Going is Gone," *Economist*, June 15, 2013.

[32] IMF, "IMF Executive Board Concludes 2012 Article IV Consultation with People's Republic of China," Public Information Notice No. 12/86, July 24, 2012, http://www.imf.org/external /np/sec/pn/2012/pn1286.htm; Simon Rabinovitch, "IMF Says Renminbi 'Moderately Undervalued'," *Financial Times*, July 25, 2012.

[33] Michael Bordo, Owen F. Humpage, Anna J. Schwartz, "Foreign-Exchange Intervention and the Fundamental Trilemma of International Finance: Notes for Currency Wars," *VoxEU*, June 18, 2012, http://www.voxeu.org/article/notes-currency

[34] U.S. Department of the Treasury, Office of International Affairs, "Report to Congress on International Economic and Exchange Rate Policies," July 8, 2010, http://www.treasury.gov /resource-center/international/exchange-ratepolicies/Documents/Foreign%20Exchange%20 Report%20July%202010.pdf.

[35] Swiss National Bank Press Release, September 6, 2011, http://www.snb.ch/en/mmr/reference /pre_20110906/source/pre_20110906.en.pdf.

[36] IMF, *International Financial Statistics*, 2013; IMF, *World Economic Outlook*, April 2013.

[37] Michael Bordo, Owen F. Humpage, Anna J. Schwartz, "Foreign-Exchange Intervention and the Fundamental Trilemma of International Finance: Notes for Currency Wars," *VoxEU*, June 18, 2012, http://www.voxeu.org/article/notes-currency

[38] Daniel Gros, "An Overlooked Currency War in Europe," *VoxEU*, October 11, 2012, http://www.voxeu.org/article/overlooked-currency

[39] Ibid., "Positive-Sum Currency Wars," *Economist*, February 14, 2013.

[40] Peter Garnham and David Oakley, "G7 Nations Co-ordinate $25bn Yen Sell-Off," *Financial Times*, March 18, 2011.

[41] According to the April 2013 Treasury report on exchange rates, the Korean government does not publish intervention data, but many market participants believe that the Korean authorities intervened in currency markets in the latter part of 2012 and early 2013. See U.S. Department of the Treasury, Office of International Affairs, "Report to Congress on International Economic and Exchange Rate Policies," April 12, 2013, http://www.treasury.gov/resourcecenter/international/exchange-rate-policies/Documents/Foreign%20Exchange%20Report%20April%202013.pdf.

[42] Alan Beattie, "Hostilities Escalate to Hidden Currency War," *Financial Times*, September 27, 2010; U.S. Department of the Treasury, Office of International Affairs, "Report to Congress on International Economic and Exchange Rate Policies," April 12, 2013, http://www.treasury.gov/resource-center/international/exchange-rate-policies/Documents/Foreign%20Exchange%20Report%20April%202013.pdf; Rebecca Howard, "NZ Central Bank Admits Currency Intervention to Dampen Dollar," *Dow Jones*, May 9, 2013.

[43] C. Fred Bergsten and Joseph E. Gagnon, "Currency Manipulation, the US Economy, and the Global Economic Order," Peterson Institute for International Economics Policy Brief 12-25, December 2012, http://www.iie.com/publications/interstitial.cfm?ResearchID=2302.

[44] Ibid.

[45] For example, see Matthew O'Brien, "Currency Wars, What Are They Good For? Absolutely Ending Depressions," *The Atlantic*, February 5, 2013; "Trial of Strength," *Economist*, September 23, 2010.

[46] For more on quantitative easing in the United States, see CRS Report R42962, *Federal Reserve: Unconventional Monetary Policy Options*, by Marc Labonte.

[47] For example, see "Brazil Warns of World Currency War," *Reuters*, September 28, 2010. In this report, exchange rate data is from the Federal Reserve unless otherwise noted.

[48] Samantha Pearson, "Brazil Launches Fresh 'Currency War' Offensive," *Financial Times*, March 15, 2012.

[49] For example, see "Phoney Currency Wars," *Economist*, February 16, 2013.

[50] U.S. Congress, Senate Banking, Housing, and Urban Affairs, *Hearing on the Semi-Annual Monetary Policy Report*, 113th Cong., 1st sess., February 26, 2013.

[51] For example, see Matthew Malinowski and Blake Schmidt, "Brazil Real Surges on $60 Billion Intervention Plan," *Bloomberg*, August 23, 2013.

[52] G-20 Leaders' Declaration, September 2013, St. Petersburg, http://www.g20.org/documents.

[53] IMF, *World Economic Outlook Update*, July 9, 2013, http://www.imf.org/external/pubs /ft/weo/2013/update/02/.

[54] Simon Kennedy and Scott Rose, "Russia Says World is Nearing Currency War as Europe Joins," *Bloomberg*, January 16, 2013.

[55] Lingling Wei, "China Fund Warns Japan Against a 'Currency War,'" *Wall Street Journal*, March 6, 2013; Cynthia Kim, "South Korea's Hyun Says Yen Bigger Issue than North Korea," *Bloomberg*, April 18, 2013.

[56] IMF, "Japan: Solid Recovery, but Europe Dampens Outlook," IMF Survey Online, June 12, 2012, http://www.imf.org/external/pubs/ft/survey/so/2012/car061112b.htm.

[57] "Japan Denies Currency Manipulation Claims Ahead of G20," *Reuters*, January 25, 2013.

[58] "Positive-Sum Currency Wars," *Economist*, February 14, 2013.

[59] IMF, "The United States Spillover Report – 2011 Article IV Consultation," IMF Country Report No. 11/203, July 2011, pp. 32, http://www.imf.org/external/pubs/ft /scr/2011/cr11203.pdf.

[60] For example, see Jeffrey Frankel, "Dispatches from the Currency Wars," *Project Syndicate*, June 11, 2013. http://www.project-syndicate.org/blog/dispatches-from-the-currency-wars.

[61] The Group of 7 (G-7) includes Canada, France, Germany, Italy, Japan, the United States, and the United Kingdom. The Group of 20 (G-20) includes the G-7 countries plus Argentina, Australia, Brazil, Canada, China, India, Indonesia, Mexico, Russia, Saudi Arabia, South Africa, South Korea, Turkey, and the European Union (EU). For more on the G20, see CRS Report R40977, *The G-20 and International Economic Cooperation: Background and Implications for Congress*, by Rebecca M. Nelson.

[62] For more on the IMF, CRS Report R42019, *International Monetary Fund: Background and Issues for Congress*, by Martin A. Weiss.

[63] For example, see Morris Goldstein, "Currency Manipulation and Enforcing the Rules of the International Monetary System," in *Reforming the IMF for the 21st Century*, ed. Edwin M. Truman, Special Report 19 ed. (Institute for International Economics, 2006), http://www.piie.com/publications/chapters_preview/3870/05iie3870.pdf.

[64] Between the end of World War II and the early 1970s, the IMF supervised a fixed exchange rate system, in which the value of all currencies was fixed to the U.S. dollar, and the value of the dollar was fixed to gold. Countries could not change their exchange rates by more than 10% without the Fund's consent, and could only do so to correct a "fundamental disequilibrium" in exchange rate values. This system broke down in the early 1970s when the United States floated its currency, and some other countries subsequently decided to float their currencies as well. After a period of turmoil in world currency markets, an amendment to the IMF's founding document—the Articles of Agreement—was adopted in

1978. This Amendment laid out member countries' obligations on exchange rate policies to incorporate the shift to floating currencies adopted by some IMF member countries.

[65] IMF Articles of Agreement (as amended), http://www.imf.org/External/Pubs/FT/AA/#art4.

[66] IMF Article IV.

[67] Effective balance of payments adjustment generally refers to a country's ability to, over time, balance its international transactions, particularly relating to the capital account (financial transactions) and its current account (export and import of goods and services, plus income and other unilateral transfers, such as gifts or remittances).

[68] IMF, "IMF Executive Board Adopts New Decision on Bilateral Surveillance over Members' Policies," Public Information Notice (PIN) No. 07/69, June 21, 2007, http://www.imf.org/external/np/sec/pn/2007/pn0769.htm; IMF, "IMF Executive Board Adopts New Decision on Bilateral and Multilateral Surveillance," Public Information Notice (PIN) No. 12/89, July 30, 2012, http://www.imf.org/external /np/sec/pn/2012/pn1289.htm.

[69] IMF Articles of Agreement, Article XXVI:2.

[70] Joseph E. Gagnon, "Combating Widespread Currency Manipulation," Peterson Institute for International Economics Policy Brief PB12-19, July 2012, http://www.iie.com/publications /pb/pb12-19.pdf.

[71] Claus D. Zimmermann, "Exchange Rate Misalignment and International Law," *The American Journal of International Law*, vol. 105, no. 3 (July 2011), pp. 423-476.

[72] Ibid.

[73] For example, see Robert W. Staiger and Alan O. Sykes, "'Currency Manipulation' and World Trade," *World Trade Review*, vol. 9, no. 4 (2010), pp. 583-627; Haneul Jung, "Tackling Currency Manipulation with International Law: Why and How Currency Manipulation Should be Adjudicated?," *Manchester Journal of International Economic Law*, vol. 9, no. 2 (2012), pp. 184-200.

[74] WTO Agreement on Subsidies and Countervailing Measures, http://www.wto.org/english /docs_e/legal_e/24- scm.pdf.

[75] GATT Article XV(4), http://www.wto.org/english/docs_e/legal_e/gatt47_01_e. htm#article XV.

[76] For example, see Aaditya Mattoo and Arvind Subramanian, "Currency Undervaluation and Sovereign Wealth Funds: A New Role for the World Trade Organization," Peterson Institute for International Economics Working Paper WP 08- 2, January 2008, http://www.petersoninstitute.org/publications/wp/wp08-2.pdf; Gary Hufbauer, Yee Wong, and Ketki Sheth, *US-China Trade Disputes: Rising Tide, Rising Stakes*. Policy Analyses in International Economics 78. Washington: Institute for International Economics, 2006; Michael Waibel, "Retaliating Against Exchange-Rate Manipulation under WTO Rules," *VoxEU*, April 16, 2010, http://www.voxeu.org/article/retaliating-against-exchangerate-manipulation-under-wto-rules.

[77] Robert E. Scott, "Currency Manipulation—History Shows that Sanctions are Needed," Economic Policy Institute, April 29, 2010, http://www.epi.org/publication/pm164/.

[78] Gregory Hudson, Pedro Bento de Faria, and Tobias Peyerl, "The Legality of Exchange Rate Undervaluation Under WTO Law," Geneva Graduate Institute, Center for Trade and Economic Integration Working Paper, July 2011, http://graduateinstitute.ch/webdav/site /ctei/shared/CTEI/working_papers/CTEI-2011-07.pdf.

[79] The Group of 7 (G-7) includes Canada, France, Germany, Italy, Japan, the United States, and the United Kingdom.

[80] The Group of 20 (G-20) includes the G-7 countries plus Argentina, Australia, Brazil, Canada, China, India, Indonesia, Mexico, Russia, Saudi Arabia, South Africa, South Korea, Turkey, and the European Union (EU). For more on the G-20, see CRS Report R40977, *The G-20 and International Economic Cooperation: Background and Implications for Congress*, by Rebecca M. Nelson.

[81] "Divine Intervention," *Economist*, March 27, 2008.

[82] P.L. 100-418; 22 U.S.C. 5301-5306.

[83] C. Randall Henning, "Congress, Treasury, and the Accountability of Exchange Rate Policy: How the 1988 Trade Act Should be Reformed," Institute for International Economics Working Paper 07-8, September 2007, http://www.iie.com/publications/wp/wp07-8.pdf.

[84] The Treasury Department also posts the currency reports on its website: http://www.treasury.gov/resourcecenter/international/exchange-rate-policies/Pages/index.aspx.

[85] Treasury cited Taiwan and South Korea in 1988 and China in 1992. Taiwan's and South Korea's citations lasted for at least two 6-month reporting periods, while China's lasted for five 6-month reporting periods. Taiwan was cited again in 1992. U.S. Government Accountability Office, *Treasury Assessments Have Not Found Currency Manipulation, but Concerns about Exchange Rates Continue*, GAO-05-351, April 2005, http://www.gao.gov/assets/250/246061.pdf.

[86] Section 221 of the Consolidated Appropriations Act, 2005 (P.L. 108-447).

[87] U.S. Government Accountability Office, *Treasury Assessments Have Not Found Currency Manipulation, but Concerns about Exchange Rates Continue*, GAO-05-351, April 2005, http://www.gao.gov/assets/250/246061.pdf.

[88] Section 1103(a)(2)(B)(iii) of the Omnibus Trade and Competitiveness Act of 1988 (P.L. 100-418).

[89] Section 2102(c)(12) of the Trade Act of 2002 (P.L. 107-210).

[90] Bank of England; News Release – G7 Statement, February 12, 2013, http://www.bankofengland.co.uk/publications/Pages/news/2013/027.aspx.

[91] Charles Clover, Robin Harding, and Alice Ross, "G20 Agrees to Avoid Currency Wars," *Financial Times*, February 17, 2013; G-20 Communiqué, Meeting of Finance Ministers and Central Bank Governors, Moscow, February 15-16, 2013, available at http://www.g20.org/documents/.

[92] G-20 Leaders' Declaration, September 2013, St. Petersburg, http://www.g20.org/documents.

[93] Vera Thorstensen, Daniel Ramos, and Caronlina Muller, "The 'Missing Link' Between the WTO and IMF," *Journal of International Economic Law*, vol. 16, no. 2 (2013), pp. 353-381.

[94] Fred Bergsten, "Currency Wars, the Economy of the United States, and Reform of the International Monetary System," Remarks at Peterson Institute for International Economics, May 16, 2013, http://www.iie.com/publications/papers/bergsten201305.pdf.

[95] For example, see Annie Lowrey, "A Tightrope on China's Currency," *New York Times*, October 22, 2012.

[96] U.S. Department of the Treasury, Office of International Affairs, "Report to Congress on International Economic and Exchange Rate Policies," April 12, 2013, http://www.treasury.gov/resource-center/international/exchange-rate-policies/Documents/Foreign%20Exchange%20Report%20April%202013.pdf.

[97] U.S. Representative Sander Levin, "U.S.-Japan Automotive Trade: Proposal to Level the Playing Field," http://www.piie.com/publications/papers/levin20130723proposal.pdf. The proposal calls for, among other things, a commitment by TPP countries to avoid

manipulating exchange rates to gain an unfair competitive advantage over other TPP countries; establishing specific benchmarks by which to determine whether a TPP country has manipulated its exchange rate; and enforcing commitments to avoid exchange rate manipulation through the normal dispute settlement mechanism of the TPP agreement.

[98] The bill provides details on how it would be determined if a country had a fundamentally undervalued currency, and the size of the real effective exchange rate undervaluation. Introduced by Representative Levin, it is similar to bills introduced by Representative Levin in the 112th Congress (H.R. 639) and in the 111th Congress (H.R. 2378). The House passed H.R. 2378 in September 2010.

[99] More generally, the bill requires the Treasury Department to issue a semiannual report to Congress on international monetary policy and exchange rates; prescribes negotiations and consultations with countries with fundamentally misaligned exchange rates, and actions to take against "priority action" countries that have failed, or persistently failed, to take action to eliminate the fundamental exchange rate misalignment; requires the Treasury Secretary to oppose any proposed changes in the international financial institutions that would increase the representation of countries with fundamentally misaligned currencies that are designated for priority action; amends countervailing and antidumping duty legislation to incorporate imports from countries with fundamentally misaligned currencies; and establishes an Advisory Committee on International Exchange Rate Policy. It would also repeal the Exchange Rates and International Economic Policy Coordination Act of 1988. Introduced by Senator Brown, this bill is similar to S. 1619, which Senator Brown introduced in the 112th Congress and was passed by the Senate in October 2011.

In: Money, Economics, and Finance. Volume 3    ISBN: 978-1-63321-505-4
Editor: Clifford Dobrowski                © 2014 Nova Science Publishers, Inc.

*Chapter 3*

# RECENT TRENDS IN CONSUMER RETAIL PAYMENT SERVICES DELIVERED BY DEPOSITORY INSTITUTIONS[*]

## *Darryl E. Getter*

## SUMMARY

Congressional interest in the performance of the credit and debit card (checking account services) markets and how recent developments are affecting customers is growing. This report discusses these developments and examines the costs and availability of consumer retail payments services, particularly those provided by depository institutions, since the recent recession and subsequent legislative actions.

Consumer retail payment services include products such as credit cards, cash advances, checking accounts, debit cards, and prepayment cards. Some depository institutions have increased fees and decreased availability of these services; many others are considering the best way to cover rising costs to provide these services without alienating customers. Recent declines in the demand for loans, a historically and persistently low interest rate environment, higher capital requirements, and the existence of potential profit opportunities in non-traditional banking markets may have motivated these reactions. In addition,

---

[*] This is an edited, reformatted and augmented version of a Congressional Research Service publication R43364, prepared for Members and Committees of Congress, dated January 16, 2014.

passage of the Credit Card Accountability Responsibility and Disclosure Act of 2009 (CARD Act; P.L. 111-24) and Section 920 of the Dodd-Frank Wall Street Reform and Consumer Protection Act of 2010 (Dodd-Frank Act; P.L. 111-203), which is known as the Durbin Amendment, placed limitations on fee income for credit cards and debit cards, respectively.

Determining the extent to which one or all of these factors have influenced changes in the consumer retail payment services markets, however, is challenging. Market outcomes are often influenced by multiple simultaneous or overlapping events, thus making it difficult to attribute the reactions of financial service providers and their customers solely to any one particular factor. Any one or all of the factors listed above that occurred after 2007 may have driven changes in the costs or availability of consumer retail payment services, making it difficult to determine which one had the greatest influence on market outcomes.

Depository institutions reduced credit card loan limits during the recent recession, but those limits have since been rising. Customers with impaired credit, however, have seen increases in credit card rates and reduced access to this product. Many large depository institutions have also discontinued debit card rewards programs and "free" checking. Many small financial institutions have not increased checking account fees as aggressively, but many have increased fees on less frequently used financial services and are considering further fee increases to cover anticipated higher costs. The consumer retail payment services market may also be growing more bifurcated. For example, customers more likely to repay obligations or maintain high checking account balances may experience few changes in costs or availability of traditional payments services. At the same time, customers likely to face higher costs to use or limited access to traditional payment services may increase their usage of direct deposit cash advances and prepayment cards, as depository institutions make these options increasingly available to this market segment.


# INTRODUCTION

The consumer retail payments system facilitates transactions to purchase goods and services, pay bills, obtain cash through withdrawals and advances, and make person-to-person payments.[1] Consumers may use cash, checks, or traditional electronic banking products to facilitate these transactions. Traditional electronic banking products include credit cards and debit cards. Revolving credit or credit cards serve as unsecured (no collateral) short-term lending for some cardholders, if the outstanding balance is not repaid in full, and a convenient way to make transactions for others, if they fully repay balances upon receipt of the billing statement. Debit cards facilitate electronic access to checking account services discussed in more detail later in this report. Debit cards are provided primarily by depository institutions (banks and credit unions), but any institution that provides checking account services may provide debit cards.

According to the Federal Reserve Payments Study, the United States has seen continued growth of noncash or electronic payments.[2] Electronic payments are made by electronic payment (credit, debit, and prepayment) cards and by the automated clearing house (ACH), an electronic network used for direct deposit and electronic bill payment. In 2009, checking account holders were more than twice as likely to choose an electronic payment option over writing checks, indicating their preference for electronic financial services.[3] Debit cards and ACH payments were used in 35% and 18%, respectively, of noncash payments; paper checks accounted for another 22% of these transactions. The remaining noncash payments were conducted using credit cards and prepayment cards at percentages of 20% and 5%, respectively. In 2012, the percentages of noncash payment transactions using debit cards, credit cards, ACH payments, paper checks, and prepayment cards were 38%, 21%, 18%, 15%, and 7%, respectively.[4] In addition to the decline in paper check writing, checks increasingly were deposited with images (from 13% of deposits in 2009 to 17% in 2012). As the payments system continues to evolve, consumers using financial retail services provided by regulated depository institutions arguably enjoy benefits (e.g., stemming from various consumer protection laws designed to protect against unfair, discriminatory, or predatory practices) that may not be associated with non-covered financial service providers.[5]

Preliminary evidence suggests that, since 2009, some consumers experienced either higher charges or less availability of retail payment services provided by depository institutions. These developments may arguably be attributed to some of the following explanations.

- After the 2007-2009 recession, the demand for consumer loans declined, and U.S. interest rates dropped to historically low levels for an abnormally long period of time.[6] Declines in lending volumes and loan yields can squeeze profit margins, perhaps motivating depository institutions to increase fees on several products and services.
- Capital requirements for non-performing loans increased for the banking system.[7] Providing traditional retail services became more

expensive for certain financial institutions with many customers
unable or unwilling to repay obligations, triggering the need to hold
greater amounts of capital in reserve against losses. Hence, depository
institutions were inclined to show greater selectivity when making
potentially costly financial products available.

- Rather than wait for the profitability to return to more traditional lines
  of business, depository institutions sought profits from emerging
  opportunities in new business lines, discussed later in this report.

- Congress passed legislation in 2009 and 2010 that placed limitations
  on fee pricing practices for credit and debit cards, discussed in greater
  detail below.[8] Disclosure requirements of remittances (electronic
  transfers of funds by a consumer to a person or business in a foreign
  country) may result in costs that some (small) depository institutions
  would not want to incur without sufficient volume to justify the
  expense.[9] Hence, the loss of fee income increases as well as other
  regulatory requirements may increase the difficulty of providing retail
  payment services at little or no cost to customers.

There is congressional interest in how the costs and availability of
consumer retail payments services provided primarily by depository
institutions have changed following the passage of recent legislative actions,
namely the Credit Card Accountability Responsibility and Disclosure Act of
2009 (CARD Act; P.L. 111-24) and Section 920 of the Dodd-Frank Wall
Street Reform and Consumer Protection Act of 2010 (Dodd-Frank Act; P.L.
111-203), which is known as the Durbin Amendment. Any one or all of the
factors listed above that occurred after 2007 may have prompted changes in
the consumer retail payment services market, making it difficult to determine
which one had the greatest influence on market outcomes. This report recounts
developments beginning in 2006 in the markets for credit cards and checking
account services delivered primarily by depository institutions.

Preliminary evidence indicates some recent segmentation of the consumer
retail payments market. Customers with the ability to repay short-term loans in
a timely manner or maintain sufficient deposit balances may notice little change
in cost or availability of traditional retail payment services. On the other hand,
customers who generate fees, such as insufficient funds fees that
simultaneously trigger increased regulatory capital costs on their depository
institutions, may find themselves paying more or experiencing limited access
to conventional retail payment services. Some depository institutions,
however, are offering this market segment greater payment services

characterized by less credit or nonpayment risks, such as direct deposit cash advances and prepayment cards. These products and services, which are also part of the consumer retail payments system, are defined and discussed later in this report.

# Recent Developments in the Credit Card Market

Congressional concerns about hidden and complex penalty fees and assessments on credit card holders led to passage of the CARD Act.[10] Various provisions of the CARD Act were implemented on August 20, 2009, and February 22, 2010, with full implementation accomplished by August 22, 2010.[11] Some notable provisions appear below.

---

**Summary of Some Key CARD Act Regulations**

- The CARD Act established circumstances when rate increases or fees on outstanding balances would be permissible.
- Advance notice (45 days) is required before any rate or fee increases.
- Accounts that experience rate increases must be reviewed every 6 months to determine if a rate reduction is warranted.
- A payment made by a cardholder with multiple accounts will be applied first to the balance with the highest rate, and then to each successive balance bearing the next highest rate until the payments are exhausted.
- A customer must receive a periodic statement within a reasonable amount of time (not less than 21 days) before payment is due.
- If a creditor changes terms, such as increasing the interest rate that would apply to future purchases, consumers must receive notice of their right to cancel the account before the effective date of the change. Cancellation of an existing account shall not trigger a demand for immediate repayment of the full amount owed or additional fees. Consumers must instead be offered a repayment option. The existing balance of a repayment option may be amortized on a schedule of not less than five years. A new repayment schedule may be established in which the percentage of the outstanding balance of the periodic repayment does not increase by more than twice the percentage required under the consumer's existing schedule.

- Enhanced consumer disclosures (e.g., the consequences of making only the minimum monthly payment, late payment deadlines and penalties, prominent disclosure of payment deadlines) are required.
- Credit card issuance to consumers under 21 years of age is limited.
- Total fees cannot exceed 25% of the initial credit limit, affecting the availability of subprime ("fee harvester") credit cards.
- Monetary penalties for violations of the Truth in Lending Act (TILA) as it relates to credit card lending were increased.

Risk-based pricing is the practice of charging riskier borrowers higher rates to reflect their additional credit or default risk.[12] Billing practices, such as double-cycle billing, served as a form of risk-based pricing of credit to cardholders immediately if their behavior indicated greater default risk. If cardholders switched from using their cards simply for transaction purposes to revolving loan purposes or missed a payment, fees and higher finance charges were imposed almost immediately, often without any grace period.

The CARD Act eliminated various billing practices and limited the ability to raise rates without providing advance notice to customers; however, there were no caps placed on credit card interest rates. Consequently, while risk-based pricing of cardholders may have been more difficult via the use of fees, credit card issuers have other available options to manage default risk. Card issuers could reduce lending risks by lowering credit limits and increasing credit card rates on all borrowers, both timely and delinquent.[13] Another response may be to increase rates and reduce limits for borrowers with greater delinquency and default risk. Issuers could also decide to limit the availability of this product to riskier customers.

Subprime credit card lending, or lending to borrowers with impaired credit, still exists; but identifying how the issuance of "fee harvester" cards has changed is difficult due to lack of available data.[14] One alternative to *unsecured* revolving credit to risky borrowers is *secured* revolving credit. Secured credit cards, which are offered to borrowers with missing or impaired credit histories, require either security deposits as collateral for the amount of the line of credit or links to checking or savings accounts, thereby allowing lenders to recover funds if payments are missed. The security deposit is refunded if borrowers do not miss payments.[15] Customer payment activity does get reported to credit bureaus. Hence, secured credit card lending can help borrowers build or repair creditworthiness. Secured credit cards would still be subject to fee limitations and disclosure regulations stemming from the CARD Act. There is some evidence suggesting that the availability of secured credit card lending has subsequently risen in light of the regulation of subprime credit card lending, but locating official data sources that distinguish between unsecured and secured credit card lending is difficult.[16]

The Federal Reserve Bank of New York (FRBNY) collected a nationally representative sample of credit report data to estimate the availability of revolving credit for consumers.[17]

Revolving credit availability and usage has declined, but estimates of the size of the decline vary depending upon the chosen time interval. Using the FRBNY data displayed in the first column of *Table 1*, household credit limits declined by 28.2% between 2008 and 2010; the decline is calculated to be 11.0% over the longer period 2006-2012.[18] The second column of *Table 1* shows the aggregate amount of revolving or credit card debt outstanding as reported by the Federal Reserve.

### Table 1. Credit Card Limits, Balances, Terms Before and After the CARD Act

| Year | Average Amount Available Credit Limit (Trillions of Dollars, FRBNY) | Amount Consumer Credit Outstanding: Revolving (Billions of Dollars, G.19) | Credit Terms (Interest Rate) Commercial Banks, Credit Card Plans: All Accounts (Percent, G.19) | Credit Terms (Interest Rate) Commercial Banks, Credit Card Plans: Accounts Assessed Interest (Percent, G.19) | Estimates of Credit Terms (Interest Rate): "Cards for Bad Credit" (Percent, CreditCards.com) |
|------|------|------|------|------|------|
| 2006 | 2.37 | 924.9 | 13.21 | 14.73 | n.a. |
| 2007 | 2.50 | 1002.9 | 13.30 | 14.68 | 13.27 |
| 2008 | 2.73 | 1005.2 | 12.08 | 13.57 | 11.86 |
| 2009 | 2.21 | 917.2 | 13.40 | 14.31 | 13.26 |
| 2010 | 1.96 | 840.7 | 13.78 | 14.26 | 21.09 |
| 2011 | 2.05 | 842.5 | 12.74 | 13.09 | 24.78 |
| 2012 | 2.11 | 845.8 | 12.06 | 12.96 | 23.64 |

Source: The data come from the following data sources: Federal Reserve Bank of New York (FRBNY) Consumer Credit Panel (http://www.newyorkfed.org/ householdcredit /2013-Q2/index.html), Board of Governors of the Federal Reserve System G.19 Statistical Release (http://www.federal reserve. gov/Releases/g19/current/ default.htm), and various CreditCards.com's Weekly Rate Reports. The particular source is indicated in parentheses. The figures are not adjusted for inflation.

Notes: Averages of the Estimated Amount Available Credit Limits were computed by CRS.

Although the amount of credit card debt outstanding declined by 16.4% between 2008 and 2010, the decline was 8.6% between 2006 and 2012. The 2008-2010 period captures the year immediately before and after passage of the CARD Act as well as the trough of the 2007-2009 recession. The 2006-2012 period captures more of the recovery following the 2007-2009 recession, thus showing less of a decline in credit card usage.

Similarly, the change in credit costs or terms (interest rates) is sensitive to the chosen time interval. Revolving credit costs increased for all accounts and for those assessed interest (carrying balances) over the 2008 and 2010 period; however, the costs actually declined over the longer 2006-2012 period of time. In 2010, the credit terms for borrowers with impaired credit spiked after a period of rising credit card defaults and subsequent accounting recognition of losses from uncollectible obligations (charge-offs) that occurred during the 2007-2009 recession.[19] These findings may reflect greater bifurcation of the credit card market into high-quality and impaired borrowing groups. These findings are consistent with the anticipated reaction by lenders to both the recession and the CARD Act.

There have recently been conflicting reports of credit card market activity in terms of cost and availability. An academic study reports that the CARD Act reduced overall borrowing costs to consumers, with no offsetting increase in interest charges or reduction in credit access over the 2008 to 2011 period.[20] The results from the academic study, however, do not appear to be consistent with various industry reports. The American Bankers Association reported in a comment letter filed with the Consumer Financial Protection Bureau that new credit card users and impaired credit card users experienced higher costs and less availability of credit card credit.[21] Given the historically and persistently low (prime) interest rate environment coupled with a decline in demand for consumer loans, banks have been looking for lending opportunities that would allow them to charge higher interest rates.[22] Consequently, small and regional banks have reportedly renewed their interest in credit card lending after some retrenchment during the recession.[23] Furthermore, the decline in outstanding consumer credit, as reported in *Table 1* by the New York Federal Reserve Bank, has not returned to pre-recession (2006) levels. The relatively lower amount of credit card usage could reflect both lower credit card loan demand as well as higher lending standards reportedly imposed by (large bank) lenders.[24]

Generally speaking, it is difficult to attribute outcomes in the credit card market solely to either the 2007-2009 U.S. recession or to the CARD Act, which simultaneously affected both the demand for and supply of revolving credit.[25] The demand for revolving credit decreased over 2008-2010, and credit card defaults, some of which may have stemmed from the recession, increased.[26] In absence of the CARD Act, outstanding credit balances along with the cost of credit for most borrowers would be expected to decline as the uncertainty generated by a severe recession would likely reduce the demand for revolving credit. Furthermore, in absence of the CARD Act, rising credit card defaults would be expected to reduce lenders' willingness to supply revolving credit. Credit card limits and loans may decline, and credit card rates for riskier borrowers would be likely to increase (if they are able to obtain any credit). The observed outcomes would still be consistent with predicted reactions to requirements stemming from the CARD Act.

## RECENT DEVELOPMENTS IN THE MARKET FOR CHECKING ACCOUNT SERVICES

Checking accounts are used by customers for deposits and to make payments. The full range of checking account services includes access to deposits via debit cards and access to ACH bill payment services, as well as any automated overdraft protection.[27] Depository institutions incur costs to provide checking account services. Interest is paid to depositors to use their funds to originate new loans.[28] Other costs associated with providing checking account services include maintenance and other regulatory requirements (e.g., monthly statements, deposit insurance, security). Recent developments in both the cost and availability of checking account services are examined in this section because overdraft and debit card fees are tied to the delivery of this financial product to customers.

The CARD Act also regulated overdraft fees.[29] An overdraft occurs when a customer's checking account does not have enough funds to cover the total amount of a purchase made with a check or debit card. Prior to the CARD Act, some depository institutions automatically enrolled its customers in an overdraft or "insufficient funds" protection program that would cover a shortage, and then charged the customer a fee. The CARD Act, however, required depository institutions to seek permission from customers before automatically enrolling them in automatic overdraft protection programs. Unless customers "opt in" or give their permission for overdraft protection, then financial institutions must reject transactions resulting in overdrafts.

When a consumer makes a purchase using a debit card, the merchant pays a "swipe" fee, of which a portion is called the *interchange fee*. The interchange fee is paid to the consumer's bank that issued the debit card to cover the costs to process the transaction, prevent fraud, and other service fees. Section 920 of the Dodd-Frank Act, known as the Durbin Amendment, required the Federal Reserve Board to issue regulations to ensure that any interchange transaction fee received by a bank (with $10 billion or more in assets that issues a debit card) is "reasonable and proportional" to the cost.[30] The Federal Reserve could consider the authorization, clearance, and settlement costs of each transaction when setting the interchange fee. The statute allows the interchange fee to be adjusted for costs incurred by debit-card issuers to prevent fraud, but the Federal Reserve may not consider other costs associated with the transaction.[31] The legislation does not regulate the interchange fees associated with reloadable prepayment cards or debit cards provided pursuant to a federal, state, or local government administered program. On June 29, 2011, the Federal Reserve issued a final rule to implement the Durbin Amendment.[32] A summary of notable requirements affecting checking account services appear below.

---

### Summary of Some Key Fee Regulations Affecting Checking Account Services

- As required by the CARD Act, Regulation E was amended to require customers to opt-in and provide affirmative consent for overdraft coverage of ATM withdrawals and non-recurring debit card transactions. The new rules do not cover checks or automatic bill payments.[33]
- The final rule implementing the Durbin Amendment does not regulate the interchange fee that a network provider may charge; it only restricts the amount of interchange fee revenue that large-issuing banks may receive. After conducting a survey to obtain transaction cost information,[34] the Federal Reserve issued a rule that caps the interchange fee received by large issuers (with $10 billion or more in assets) to 21 cents plus 0.05% of the transaction. The Federal Reserve also allows for a 1 cent adjustment if the issuer implements fraud-prevention standards that satisfy the requirements set out in an interim final rule.[35]

---

Free or low-cost checking at depository institutions has reportedly diminished, primarily at large depository institutions, which may reflect substitution into new fee generating strategies since previous strategies became less viable after 2007.[36] For example, fee income, which was generated by the sale of mortgage loans to the private-label mortgage securitization market, declined after investors deserted the market at the beginning of the financial crisis.[37] The difficulty to generate fees increased following the decline in overall customer demand for loans and other traditional banking services after 2007. New regulations limiting credit card fees, overdraft fees, and the amount of fees that large institutions could collect from debit transactions were also in place by 2011. Previous fee generating activities may have been used to cross-subsidize or reduce the total costs of providing financial services to customers, allowing many services to be offered for a nominal charge or free.[38] Given the fading away of these revenue generating options, more financial institutions may be pursuing new fee pricing strategies, which includes customers covering more of the costs of checking account services.[39]

Industry reports indicate that checking account services have become more expensive for those depositors unable to maintain balances above specified minimums or who fail to incur fees via use of multiple financial services. Rather than charge higher monthly maintenance fees to all customers, many pricing strategies allow depositors the option to maintain relatively larger account balances or use multiple financial services to avoid fees.[40] Small depository institutions, which are more dependent upon deposits to carry out their functions, reportedly have not been as aggressive as large banks to increase checking account fees.[41] Nevertheless, both large and small depository institutions are considering pricing strategies to replace revenue streams that may have disappeared in a manner that does not alienate their more profitable customers.[42]

In addition to higher fees, various checking account services reportedly became less available to customers as they become more costly to service. Overdraft protection service is analogous to a cash advance or payday loan that lacks any underwriting.[43] Similarly, when an overdraft is not covered by the customer within 60 days, banks are required to treat those balances as charge-offs, meaning that the obligations must be recognized as uncollectible and charged against allowances for loan and lease losses (ALLL) reserves.[44] Thus, the severe economic downturn incentivized depository institutions to reduce overdraft limits for the same reason credit card limits were reduced. Institutions had to set aside greater amounts of current income to absorb losses, which reduced profits even more at a time when interest rates were historically low and fee restrictions were implemented. Hence, *involuntary* checking account closures have allegedly increased, prompting increased reporting to banking history bureaus of overdraft and insufficient funds activity.[45] If involuntary closures reflect activity associated with a disproportionate amount of low-income individuals, then this group may encounter difficulties gaining access to traditional checking account services for several years.[46]

Many banks covered by the Durbin Amendment eliminated their debit card rewards programs after implementation, but this simultaneously eliminated a mode for attracting (checking account) deposits to fund loans.[47] Offering checking accounts with direct deposit, automated bill paying, and debit card services helps depository institutions attract customers that are likely to use other financial products, including loan products. Furthermore, when customers use a variety of financial products and services, the ability of a depository institution to cross-subsidize its costs and financial risks is enhanced. Given that financial institutions are still interested in attracting deposits, many of them have entered into partnerships with merchants who are sponsoring more customer reward programs.[48] The customer gets rewards for shopping with a particular merchant and paying for their purchases using an electronic payment card (i.e., credit, debit, or prepayment card) associated with a particular bank.[49]

In addition to Durbin Amendment fee restrictions, capital buffers for non-performing loans increased for the banking system as a result of enhanced capital requirements.[50] Both factors would prompt less willingness to tolerate less profitable or more expensive customers. Depository institutions would be incentivized to separate customers into two categories: those who generate fee income using a variety of financial products, and those who primarily generate overdraft and insufficient funds fees, which trigger higher regulatory capital costs.

## ALTERNATIVES TO TRADITIONAL RETAIL PAYMENT SERVICES

Financial products commonly used by unbanked populations have experienced recent popularity among people no longer able to qualify for traditional banking products, particularly if they have recently defaulted on loans.[51] Depository institutions have reportedly demonstrated a willingness to serve this market segment by offering a different set of financial services.[52] Unlike traditional relationship banking, which generally refers to a business strategy in which close familiarity or long-term relationships are developed with customer bases, depository institutions can provide a limited range of retail services with less information about how these customers manage their financial affairs.[53] The financial services associated with serving this market segment may have one or more of the following characteristics:

- the fees are required to be paid up front;
- the costs of a financial product, such as a short-term cash advance, are expensive relative to a loan arrangement expected to last for a year or longer;[54]
- any information pertaining to customer payment history is unlikely to be reported to any credit bureau;
- a formal or long-term relationship with a traditional depository institution is not required to obtain alternative financial services.

## Direct Deposit Cash Advances

Depository institutions periodically change the delivery or format of their payday loan (cash advance) products.[55] Subprime credit cards and overdraft coverage for checking accounts have features analogous to payday loans, and are considered substitutes. Direct deposit or salary cash advances, a more recent version of the payday loan service, is arguably a close substitute for fee harvester credit cards and overdraft coverage products.[56] Direct deposit cash advances, similar to payday loans, are not underwritten. Customers must be employed and must set up direct deposit with their checking accounts. The fees charged for this financial product would not be considered overdraft fees, and they are not associated with a credit card. Regulations for the credit card and checking account products, therefore, are not directly applicable to the direct deposit cash advance product. The design of this cash advance product allows depository institutions to serve the 'overdraft' market segment while generating new revenue streams in lieu of defunct fee-income streams.[57]

Payment of a direct deposit cash advance is due in approximately 30 days, in contrast to a credit card loan that is typically underwritten based upon a one-year period.[58] Thus, the annual percentage rate (APR) computation for a direct deposit cash advance is likely to be significantly greater than for a loan designed to be repaid over a period of years.[59] Also, customer payment histories are not reported to any credit bureaus. Hence, customers could use this product if they are unable to qualify for a traditional credit card.[60]

Publicly available data on payday lending are scarce, and data on the various forms of payday lending conducted by financial institutions are scarcer. Various reports indicate that large institutions are offering deposit advance products, and that federal regulators have heightened scrutiny of this activity.[61] For example, the Consumer Financial Protection Bureau (CFPB) conducted a 12-month study over 2012 that included a small number of depository institutions that offered direct deposit account advances, with a common loan limit of $500.[62] In addition, the Office of the Comptroller of the Currency (OCC) and the Federal Deposit Insurance Corporation (FDIC), which are federal banking regulatory agencies that focus on activities posing bank solvency risks issued final supervisory guidance regarding the delivery of these products.[63]

Federal banking regulators have expressed concerns about payday lending by banking institutions. According to the CFPB, consumers that use deposit advance products were more likely to have had overdraft transactions or incurred insufficient funds fees. Offering deposit advances, however, allows financial institutions to serve this market segment without necessarily having to increase ALLL. Consequently, the federal banking regulators expressed concern that this service, via its high costs and repeated extensions of credit, could add to borrower credit (default) risks. In addition to reminding banks of their vulnerability to various risks (e.g., credit, reputational, legal) and potential compliance violations (e.g., Truth in Lending Act, Truth in Savings Act, Equal Credit Opportunity Act, Electronic Funds Transfer Act), the agencies listed their expectations with respect to loan classification policies, underwriting and administration policies, the length of customer relationships, and customer credit histories. The guidances recommended the following: customers with impaired credit should not be eligible for this product, each deposit advance should be repaid in full before extension of a subsequent advance loan, and no more than one loan may be offered per monthly statement cycle. In light of these guidances, banks may decide to discontinue offering this financial service.[64]

## Prepayment Cards

Usage of non-cash prepayment cards, which may be considered an alternative to a traditional checking account, has reportedly increased since 2009.[65] Some prepayment cards are closed-loop, meaning that they can be used only with a specific merchant or merchants; others are open-loop, meaning that a customer can them use anywhere that accepts payment from a network provider such as Visa or MasterCard. Prepayment cards may be obtained online or in retail stores, and cash may also be loaded onto the cards at these locations. Thus, there is no need to go to a traditional bank or credit union in order to gain access to this financial product. Nevertheless, some prepayment cards can be issued with an account and routing numbers, making it possible to have payroll checks deposited directly onto the card.

Prepayment cards, however, are not perfect substitutes for checking accounts because they have relatively limited functionality. General use prepayment cards are issued to the cardholder prior to funds being loaded on the card and, unlike checking accounts, there is typically a charge for customers to "reload" cards (replenish fund balances).[66] More importantly, a prepayment card is exempted from Durbin Amendment rules as long as it is "the only means of access to the underlying funds, except when all remaining funds are provided to the cardholder in a single transaction."[67] In other words, prepayment cards cannot be attached to checking accounts, meaning that funds may not be provided by check, ACH payments, or wire transfers. Furthermore, the funds on prepayment cards generally are not federally insured like checking account deposits, and financial institutions would not have access to funds stored on those cards to make new loans.[68]

The limited functionality of prepayment cards means that they also lack some of the benefits associated with more traditional banking products. For example, prepayment cards cannot be used to repair credit given that historical records regarding usage are not maintained or reported to credit bureaus.[69] Customers also do not depend upon one primary institution to obtain prepayment cards, meaning that development of a long-term relationship with a financial firm is not necessary to make effective use of the product. Anyone unable (e.g., due to poor banking history) or unwilling to establish a relationship with a mainstream bank or credit union may use prepayment cards, which can still generate a revenue stream for issuers even if the product does not attract new long-term deposits.

Prepayment cards, therefore, enable depository institutions to provide financial services to people that prefer not to have a formal relationship with mainstream financial institutions.[70] According to a study conducted by the FDIC and the U.S. Census Bureau, 68.8% of U.S. households were "fully banked" in 2011.[71] Households in the survey were considered fully banked if they had a bank account and had not relied upon any alternative financial services (AFS) providers for a year or more.[72] People that are not fully banked, however, still need electronic payment cards for various transactions (e.g., to purchase airplane tickets, make hotel reservations). In light of consumer demand for electronic payment cards, some depository institutions appear to be aggressively seeking to enter this market. Entry into this non-traditional banking market may allow depository institutions to serve customers no longer eligible for traditional banking products. Revenues generated from expansion into the market for prepayment card services may also help offset losses stemming from fee limitations.

Federal regulators have reported on the rapid growth of banks in the prepayment card industry. On June 28, 2011, the OCC issued guidance pertaining to risk management and sound practice for national banks.[73] The OCC reminded banks to carefully monitor the risks (e.g., electronic funds transfer, fraud, reputation), especially with respect to the behavior of third party providers, as well as to ensure proper implementation of consumer disclosure policies. Similarly, the CFPB also reported that prepayment cards were the fastest growing payment instrument in the United States.[74] On May 23, 2012, the CFPB requested comments after announcing that it intends to extend consumer protections associated with electronic funds transfer activities (Regulation E) to prepayment cards.[75]

# End Notes

[1] For a broader understanding of the U.S. payments system, see CRS Report R41529, Supervision of U.S. Payment, Clearing, and Settlement Systems: Designation of Financial Market Utilities (FMUs), by Marc Labonte.

[2] The Federal Reserve Payments conducts a payment study every three years. See http://www.frbservices.org/fedfocus/ archive_perspective/perspective_0313_01.html, which also includes links to the 2001, 2004, 2007, and 2010 Federal Reserve Payment Studies.

[3] See The 2010 Federal Reserve Payments Study: Noncash Payment Trends in the United States: 2006-2009 at http://www.frbservices.org/files/communications/pdf/press/2010_payments_study.pdf and Jeremy M. Simon, "Paper to Plastic: Checks and Cash Losing to Debit and Credit," at http://www.creditcards.com/credit-card-news/debit-creditcard-preferred-payment-1271.php.

[4] See The 2013 Federal Reserve Payments Study: Noncash Payment Trends in the United States: 2006-2009 at http://www.frbservices.org/files/communications/pdf/research/2013_ pay ments_study_summary.pdf.

[5] See Maude Toussaint-Comeau and Sherrie L. W. Rhine, Increasing Participation in Mainstream Financial Markets by Black Households, Federal Reserve Bank of Chicago, Policy Studies: Consumer Issues Research Series, Chicago, IL, December 2000, http://www. Chica gofed.org/digital_assets/others/region/cedric/papers/cca-2000-4.pdf.

[6] According to the National Bureau for Economic Research, the economy was in recession most recently between December 2007 and June 2009. See http://www.nber. org/cycles/recessions.html.

[7] On July 9, 2013, federal banking regulators required an increase in bank capital (150% risk weight) to the outstanding balance of non-performing consumer loans. See CRS Report R42744, U.S. Implementation of the Basel Capital Regulatory Framework, by Darryl E. Getter.

[8] See CRS Report RL34393, The Credit Card Market: Recent Trends and Regulatory Actions, by Darryl E. Getter; and CRS Report R41913, Regulation of Debit Interchange Fees, by Darryl E. Getter.

[9] See http://files.consumerfinance.gov/f/201305_cfpb_remittance-transfer-rule_summary.pdf and CRS Report R43217, Remittances: Background and Issues for Congress, by Martin A. Weiss.

[10] For example, see Martin H. Bosworth, "Credit Card Fees Rise, Disclosure Statements Inadequate," at http://www.consumeraffairs.com/news04/2006/10/gao_credit_cards.html and Anita Hamilton, "Exposing the Credit-Card Fine Print," at http://www.time.com/time/printout/0,8816,1715293,00.html#.

[11] See http://www.philadelphiafed.org/bank-resources/publications/consumer-compliance-outlook/2010/first-quarter/ regulation-z-rules.cfm, http://www.federalreserve.gov/ news events/press/bcreg/20090715a.htm, and http://edocket.access.gpo.gov/2010/pdf/2010-624.pdf (final rule).

[12] For discussions about how the increased use of risk-based pricing strategies led to fewer credit denials and greater credit accessibility for higher risk borrowers, see Raphael W. Bostic, "Trends in Equal Access to Credit Products," in The Impact of Public Policy on Consumer Credit, eds. Thomas Durkin and Michael Staten, Massachusetts: Kluwer Academic Publishers, 2002, pp. 171-202; Wendy M. Edelberg, "Risk-based Pricing of Interest Rates in Household Loan Markets," Finance and Economics Discussion Series 2003-62. Washington: Board of Governors of the Federal Reserve System, 2003; Wendy M. Edelberg, "Risk-based Pricing of Interest Rates for Consumer Loans," Journal of Monetary Economics, vol. 53, November 2006, pp. 2283-2298; Mark Furletti and Christopher Ody, "Another Look at Credit Card Pricing and Its Disclosure: Is the Semi-Annual Pricing Data Reported by Credit Card Issuers to the Fed Helpful to Consumers or Researchers?", Payment Cards Center Discussion Paper, Federal Reserve Bank of Philadelphia, July 2006; Kathleen W. Johnson, "Recent Developments in the Credit Card Market and the Financial Obligations Ratio," Federal Reserve Bulletin, vol. 91, September 2005, pp. 473-486.

[13] Economic theory, specifically the law of supply, suggests that firms are less willing to supply products to the marketplace at lower prices. For studies on the regulatory effects of credit card rates and fees, see Diane Ellis, "The Effect of Consumer Interest Rate Deregulation on Credit Card Volumes, Charge-offs, and the Personal Bankruptcy Rate," Bank Trends, FDIC Division of Insurance, March 1998, at http://www.fdic.gov/bank/analytical/bank/bt_9805.html; and Jonathan M. Orszag and Susan H. Manning, An Economic Assessment of Regulating Credit Card Fees and Interest Rates, a study commissioned by the American Bankers Association, at http://www.aba.com/aba/ documents/press/ regulating_creditcard_fees_interest_rates92507.pdf.

[14] Fee harvester cards refer to a type of subprime credit card in which the total fees amount to a large proportion of the credit limit, making it similar in characteristics to a payday loan. On July 20, 2011, a lawsuit was filed, which challenged the application of fee limitation provisions of the CARD Act prior to opening the account. On April 12, 2012, the Consumer Financial Protection Bureau subsequently proposed a rule stating that credit card fee limitations will apply the first year after the account has been opened. The rule became effective on March 22, 2013. See http://www.consumerfinance.gov/newsroom/consumer-

financial-protection-bureau-finalizes-credit-card-act-rule/,        http://files.consumerfinance.
gov/f/201303_cfpb_final-rule_regulation-z-amendment.pdf,      and      http://online.wsj.com/
news/articles/SB10001424052702304356604577339851223075134.

[15] Unlike a prepayment card, which is defined later in the report, the customer must reload the
card once the funds are spent in order to continue using it.

[16] See  http://www.nytimes.com/2010/12/13/business/13credit.html?pagewanted=all&_r=0  and
http://www.americanbanker.com/issues/174_7/-370455-
1.html?zkPrintable=1&nopagination=1. Lending institutions are reportedly making greater
use of secured credit cards to help distinguish those defaulters that had a strong credit
record prior to the 2007-2009 recession from those who are just poor risks, suggesting that
secured credit card lending may be rising.

[17] See  http://www.newyorkfed.org/research/national_economy/householdcredit/ DistrictReport_
Q32011.pdf.

[18] See Meta Brown, Andrew Haughwout, and Donghoon Lee et al., The Financial Crisis at the
Kitchen Table: Trends in Household Debt and Credit, Federal Reserve Bank of New York,
Staff Report No. 480, New York, NY, December 2010, p. 8, http://newyorkfed.
org/research/staff_reports/sr480.pdf. A study using data from Visa, Inc. revealed that 70%
of credit line downsizing took place on dormant/inactive accounts. See Susan Herbst-
Murphy, Trends and Preferences in Consumer Payments: Lessons from the Visa Payment
Panel Study, Federal Reserve Bank of Philadelphia, Payment Cards Center Discussion
Paper, Philadelphia, PA, May 2010, p. 3, http://www.phil.frb.org/ payment-cards-
center/publications/discussion-papers/2010/D-2010-Visa-Payment-Panel-Study.pdf.

[19] Data for credit card borrowers with impaired credit were provided by Creditcards.com at
http://www.creditcard.com.

[20] See Sumit Agarwal, Souphala Chomsisengphet, and Neale Mahoney, et al., Regulating
Consumer Financial Products: Evidence from Credit Cards, National Bureau of Economic
Research, Working Paper 19484, Cambridge, MA, September 2013, http://www.nber.
org/papers/w19484; and  http://www.nytimes.com/2013/11/08/business/ economy/a-credit-
card-rule-that-worked-for-consumers.html?pagewanted=1&_r=2&pagewanted=all&.    The
study used panel data consisting of over 150 million credit card accounts and covers the
second quarter of 2008 to the fourth quarter of 2011.

[21] See  https://www.aba.com/Advocacy/commentletters/Documents/clCardAct2013Feb.pdf and
http://www.creditcards.com/credit-card-news/aba-bankers-association-card-act-1282.php.

[22] See  http://online.wsj.com/news/articles/SB10001424052748704094704575443402132987676
and    http://www.creditcards.com/credit-card-news/interest-rate-report-041713-unchanged-
2121.php.

[23] See    http://www.americanbanker.com/issues/178_142/small-banks-squeezed-to-death-reem
brace-cards-1060846- 1.html and http://www.americanbanker. com/ issues/178_179/
regional-banks-eager-to-return-to-credit-card-issuance1062090-1.html.

[24] See    http://www.americanbanker.com/issues/178_31/credit_card_lenders_keep_   getting_
pickier-1056750-1.html.

[25] See  http://blogs.reuters.com/reuters-money/2011/03/02/dont-blame-card-act-for-higher-rates-
study/.

[26] See CRS Report R41623, U.S. Household Debt Reduction, by Darryl E. Getter.

[27] The FDIC reports that overdraft protection services were more likely to be offered by larger
banking firms. Overdraft coverage limits also tended to be larger for larger banks relative to
smaller banks. The median credit limit for automated overdraft coverage was approximately

$500. See FDIC Study of Bank Overdraft Programs at http://www.fdic.gov/bank/analytical/overdraft/FDIC138_Report_Final_v508.pdf.

[28] The report refers to checking accounts, but the product may actually be a Negotiable Order of Withdrawal (NOW) account, which came about as a result of the regulation of interest rates on Demand Deposit Accounts (DDA). See http://www.consumerfinance.gov/askcfpb/953/what-difference-between-checking-account-demand-deposit-accountand-now-negotiable-order-withdrawal-account.html.

[29] Regulation E (Electronic Fund Transfers) Section 226.5 overdraft line of credit accessed by a debit card. See http://www.gpo.gov/fdsys/pkg/FR-2010-02-22/pdf/2010-624.pdf.

[30] Bank debit card issuers with less than $10 billion in assets were exempt from the regulation, allowing smaller financial institutions to receive larger interchange fees for transactions.

[31] See http://www.crs.gov/LegalSidebar/details.aspx?ID=624&Source=search.

[32] The legislation also prohibited network providers (Visa, MasterCard, etc.) and debit card issuers from imposing restrictions that would override a merchant's choice of the network provider through which to route transactions. Every issuer regardless of size is also required to link with at least two unaffiliated network providers, thus allowing merchants to choose the network provider with the lowest fees to process their debit card transactions.

[33] See http://www.federalreserve.gov/consumerinfo/wyntk_overdraft.htm and http://www. Federalreserve.gov/ newsevents/press/bcreg/20091112a.htm.

[34] See http://www.federalreserve.gov/newsevents/press/bcreg/20101216a.htm and http://edocket. access.gpo.gov/2010/ pdf/2010-32061.pdf. The Federal Reserve reported an average interchange fee of 44 cents per transaction and a median total processing cost of 11.9 cents per transaction for all debit transactions in the proposed rule. On December 16, 2010, the Federal Reserve proposed a cap of 12 cents per transaction, which only considered authorization, clearing, and settlement costs. Fraud prevention expense had not been incorporated in the proposed rule.

[35] See http://www.federalreserve.gov/newsevents/press/bcreg/20110629a.htm and http://www. federalreserve.gov/ newsevents/press/bcreg/bcreg20110629b1.pdf. For example, suppose a customer makes a $38 purchase, which is the average debit card transaction in 2009 reported by the Federal Reserve. Under the rule, the interchange fee received by the bank would be 21 cents plus 0.05% (approximately 2 cents) for a total of 23 cents. If the bank's fraud protection measures are deemed sufficient by regulators, the bank may receive an additional 1 cent for a total of 24 cents. The equivalent interchange fee for a $100 transaction would be 27 cents, or 21 cents plus 0.05% (5 cents) and 1 additional cent. The interim final rule concerning the fraud-prevention standards may be found at http://www.federalreserve.gov/ newsevents/press/bcreg/bcreg20110629a1.pdf. Whether the cap was set "too high," meaning that the Federal Reserve incorporated some fixed costs to provide debit card services that were not permitted by statute, is currently being challenged. See http://online.wsj.com/news/articles/SB10001424127887324619504579 02707291 0241080 and http://paymentsjournal.com/Content/Featured_Stories/18202/.

[36] See http://www.americanbanker.com/issues/178_161/free-checking-accounts-dwindle-at-brick-and-mortar-bankssurvey-1061458-1.html and http://www.money-rates.com/research-center/bank-fees/.

[37] For information on securitization markets issues, see U.S. Congress, Senate Committee on Banking, Housing, and Urban Affairs, Subcommittee on Securities, Insurance and Investment, Securitization of Assets: Problems and Solutions, Testimony of George P. Miller, American Securitization Forum, 111th Cong., 1st sess., October 7, 2009.

[38] In 2011, a survey found that small banks incur between $175 and $200 to offer checking account services; large banks with more than $5 billion in deposits incur between $350 and $450 in costs. See http://www.americanbanker.com/bankthink/bank-of-america-debit-interchange-durbin-1042689-1.html.

[39] See http://online.wsj.com/news/articles/SB10001424052748704070768045761815 6356154 0554.

[40] See http://www.americanbanker.com/bulletins/-1031145-1.html.

[41] See http://www.americanbanker.com/issues/178_216/small-banks-taking-serious-look-at-adding-fees-1063484- 1.html?ET=americanbanker:e17626:805795a:&st=email &utm_source=editorial&utm_medium=email& utm_campaign=AB_Daily_Briefing_110713; and http://online.wsj.com/news/ articles/ SB10001424052702304672404579182183365345064.

[42] See http://www.americanbanker.com/issues/178_25/service-charges-starting-to-rebound-at-community-banks1056475-1.html.

[43] See http://www.federalreserve.gov/boarddocs/SRLETTERS/2005/SR0503a1.pdf.

[44] Ibid. The ALLL is a component of regulatory capital that is funded with current income and must be adjusted quarterly when loan default risks increase. For more information, see CRS Report R43002, Financial Condition of Depository Banks, by Darryl E. Getter; and CFPB Study of Overdraft Programs at http://files.consumerfinance.gov/f/ 201306_cfpb_whitepaper_overdraft-practices.pdf.

[45] See http://dealbook.nytimes.com/2013/07/30/over-a-million-are-denied-bank-accounts-for-past-errors/?_r=0. Defaulted borrowers can be reported to credit history firms; similarly, frequent checking account holders that do not pay overdraft and insufficient funds fees are reported to banking history repositories, such as ChexSystems. See https://www.consumer debit.com/consumerinfo/us/en/chexsystems/faqs.htm#FAQ_01.

[46] A report regarding the mishandling of a checking account may remain on file for five years. See https://www.consumerdebit.com/consumerinfo/us/en/chexsystems/faqs.htm#FAQ_03.

[47] See http://www.creditcards.com/credit-card-news/debit-card-rewards-program-cutback-tips-1277.php, and http://www.accountingweb.com/topic/accounting-auditing/debit-cards-rewards-may-be-gone-more-changes-coming Unlike deposits, customer funds loaded on prepayment cards cannot be used by depository institutions to fund loans.

[48] See http://www.firstdata.com/downloads/thought-leadership/FI_Loyalty_WP.pdf.

[49] Advocates favoring the Durbin Amendment argued that capping interchange fees would translate into lower costs to merchants that could be passed on to consumers. The extent to which consumers see any greater benefit when merchants rather than banks have more control over customer rewards programs is ambiguous. The benefits to patrons depend more upon the generosity of the loyalty programs they use more frequently.

[50] On July 9, 2013, federal banking regulators required banks to apply a risk weight of 150% to the outstanding balance of non-performing consumer loans, which is a new requirement stemming from Basel III implementation in the United States. See CRS Report R42744, U.S. Implementation of the Basel Capital Regulatory Framework, by Darryl E. Getter.

[51] See 2011 FDIC National Survey of Unbanked and Underbanked Households at http://www.fdic.gov/ householdsurvey/2012_unbankedreport.pdf.

[52] See http://www.forbes.com/sites/halahtouryalai/2012/12/14/walmart-vs-big-banks-the-battle-for-poor-customers/.

[53] See http://www.americanbanker.com/bankthink/there-will-be-blood-the-era-of-engagement-banking-1060723- 1.html.

[54] Between December 2007 and December 2009, the FDIC conducted a small-dollar loan pilot program with 31 banks to observe the feasibility of offering lower credit cost alternatives to

payday loans and fee-based overdraft programs. (See http://www.fdic.gov/bank/ analytical/quarterly/2010_vol4_2/FDIC_Quarterly_Vol4No2_SmallDollar.pdf.) A lesson learned was that small-dollar lending programs may be successful when associated with and fostering long-term relationship lending, but it is expensive when not targeted to existing customers. See http://www.americanbanker.com/ issues/178_146/five-reasons-why-small-dollar-credit-is-so-expensive-1060965-1.html?zkPrintable=1&nopagination=1.

[55] The Federal Trade Commission defines payday lending as a cash advance by a personal check or electronic transfer. See http://www.consumer.ftc.gov/articles/0097-payday-loans. The Consumer Financial Protection Bureau defines payday lending as a cash advance in which the lender has access to the customer checking account. See http://www.consumerfinance. gov/askcfpb/search?selected_facets=category_exact:payday-loans.

[56] For more information on deposit advance products, see Payday Loans and Deposit Advance Products at http://files.consumerfinance.gov/f/201304_cfpb_payday-dap-whitepaper.pdf.

[57] See http://www.consumerfinance.gov/askcfpb/1103/my-bank-offers-direct-deposit-advance-or-checking-accountadvance-what.html.

[58] See http://www.federalreserve.gov/creditcard/#.

[59] The computation of an APR for a payday loan is arguably misleading given that the APR is an annual measurement of the interest costs. The APR is arguably a more meaningful measure for loans typically expected to be outstanding for at least one year, allowing the fixed costs to borrowers to be diffused over longer periods of time. See http://aprexplained.com/what-is-apr/ and http://www.federalreserve.gov/boarddocs/caletters/2008/0805/08- 05_attachment1.pdf.

[60] See letter written by the American Bankers Association to the Consumer Financial Protection Board at https://www.aba.com/Advocacy/commentletters/Documents/cl CardAct 2013 Feb.pdf.

[61] Six banks, four large and two regional, reportedly have offered direct deposit advances. See http://www.americanbanker.com/issues/178_80/new-regs-could-wipe-out-bank-payday-loans-1058655-1.html, http://www.npr.org/2013/04/25/179052559/regulators-warn-banks-on-direct-deposit-loans, and http://www.creditcards.com/credit-card-news/bank-advance-direct-deposit-loan-cfpb-1282.php.

[62] See http://files.consumerfinance.gov/f/201304_cfpb_payday-dap-whitepaper.pdf. The $500 limit offered with the direct deposit cash advance is similar to the median credit limit for overdraft protection as reported in the FDIC Study of Bank Overdraft Programs.

[63] Both agencies issued guidances on April 25, 2012. See http://www.occ.gov/news-issuances/news-releases/2013/nrocc-2013-69.html and http://www.fdic.gov/ news/news/ press/2013/pr13031.html. The FDIC released a final rule on direct deposit advances on November 21, 2013. See http://www.fdic.gov/news/news/press/2013/pr13105a.pdf?source= govdelivery&utm_medium=email&utm_source=govdelivery.

[64] See http://www.americanbanker.com/issues/178_225/banks-deposit-advance-guidelines-will-help-payday-lendershurt-consumers-1063840-1.html?zkPrintable=1&nopagination=1.

[65] See The Pew Charitable Trusts, Loaded With Uncertainty: Are Prepaid Cards a Smart Alternative to Checking Accounts?, Washington, DC, September 2012, at http://www.pewstates.org/research/reports/loaded-with-uncertainty85899415043.

[66] As more customers experience increases in fees for their checking account services, the ability to distinguish between prepayment cards and checking accounts on the basis of whether fees are charged is arguably becoming more difficult.

[67] See http://www.federalreserve.gov/paymentsystems/regii-faqs.htm.

[68] See http://www.fdic.gov/consumers/consumer/information/ncpw/cardstopten.html.

[69] See http://www.creditcards.com/credit-card-news/help/9-things-you-need-to-know-about-prepaid-cards-6000.php and http://www.netbanker.com/2013 /08/new_ online_ banking _report_published_new_opportunities_with_prepaid_gift_cards.html.

[70] Mainstream institutions may also be hesitant to enter into formal relationships with people with past payment problems or who have in the past incurred frequent overdrafts.

[71] See http://www.fdic.gov/householdsurvey/2012_unbankedreport_execsumm.pdf.

[72] AFS include non-bank money orders, non-bank check cashing, non-bank remittances, payday loans, pawn shops, rent-to-own stores, and refund anticipation loans.

[73] See http://www.occ.gov/news-issuances/bulletins/2011/bulletin-2011-27.html.

[74] See http://www.consumerfinance.gov/newsroom/consumer-financial-protection-bureau-considers-rules-on-prepaidcards/ and http://files.consumerfinance.gov/f/ 201205_ cfpb_GPRcards_ANPR.pdf.

[75] P.L. 90-321 Electronic Fund Transfer Act of 1978. (P.L. 95-630; 92 Stat. 3728).

In: Money, Economics, and Finance. Volume 3     ISBN: 978-1-63321-505-4
Editor: Clifford Dobrowski                © 2014 Nova Science Publishers, Inc.

*Chapter 4*

# FINANCIAL CONDITION OF DEPOSITORY BANKS[*]

## *Darryl E. Getter*

## SUMMARY

A bank is an institution that obtains either a federal or state charter that allows it to accept federally insured deposits and pay interest to depositors. In addition, the charter allows banks to make residential and commercial mortgage loans; provide check cashing and clearing services; underwrite securities that include U.S. Treasuries, municipal bonds, commercial paper, and Fannie Mae and Freddie Mac issuances; and other activities as defined by statute.

Congressional interest in the financial conditions of depository banks or the commercial banking industry has increased in the wake of the financial crisis that unfolded in 2007-2009, which resulted in a large increase in the number of distressed institutions. A financially strained banking system would have difficulty making credit available to facilitate macroeconomic recovery.

The financial condition of the banking industry can be examined in terms of profitability, lending activity, and capitalization levels (to buffer against the financial risks). This report focuses primarily on profitability and lending activity levels.

---

[*] This is an edited, reformatted and augmented version of a Congressional Research Service publication R43002, prepared for Members and Committees of Congress, dated March 26, 2014.

The banking industry continues consolidating, with more total assets held by a smaller total number of institutions. There are fewer problem banks since the peak in 2011, as well as fewer bank failures in 2013 in comparison to the peak amount of failures in 2010. Non-current loans still exceed the capacity of the banking industry to absorb potential losses (should they become uncollectible), meaning that news of industry profitability should be tempered by the news that aggregate loan loss provisions are currently insufficient. Consequently, the rate of bank lending growth may not return to pre-crisis levels until loan-loss capacity exhibits even more improvement.

# INTRODUCTION

Financial intermediation is the process of matching savers, who are willing to lend funds to earn a future rate of return, with borrowers, who are presently in need of funds to make transactions. It is expensive for savers to locate, underwrite, and monitor repayment behavior of borrowers. Similarly, it is expensive for borrowers to locate a sufficient amount of savers with funds and favorable lending terms. Hence, banks develop expertise in *intermediation*, or facilitating the transfer of funds from savers to borrowers. Although other institutions (e.g., credit unions, insurance companies, pension funds, hedge funds) also engage in the financial intermediation matching process, this report examines how depository banks are faring in this activity.

A commercial or depository bank is typically a corporation that obtains either a federal or state charter to accept federally insured deposits and pay interest to depositors; make residential and commercial mortgage loans; provide check cashing and clearing services; and may underwrite securities that include U.S. Treasuries, municipal bonds, Fannie Mae and Freddie Mac issuances, and commercial paper (unsecured short-term loans to cover short-term liquidity needs). The permissible activities of depository banks are defined by statute.[1]

The typical intermediation transaction made by banks consists of providing loans to borrowers at higher rates than the cost to borrow the funds from savers, who provide loanable funds in the form of bank deposits. Banks profit from the *spread* between the rates they receive from borrowers and the rates they pay to depositors. Facilitation of the intermediation transaction involves risk. Banks face the risk that borrowers can default on their loans, making it more difficult to repay depositors. In addition, banks face funding or liquidity risk stemming from more frequent movements in short-term interest rates. Banks must have access to an uninterrupted source of short-term funding (deposits) until their long-term loans are fully repaid, which is explained in more detail later in this report, and fluctuations in short rates translates into fluctuations in their profit spreads. Furthermore, depositors could suddenly and simultaneously decide to withdraw their deposits, perhaps due to a sudden change in economic conditions or even speculation about deteriorating economic conditions, resulting in financial distress for a bank or several banks.[2] Hence, bank profitability and financial risk are inextricably linked.

In addition to default and funding risks, financial intermediation increases the vulnerability of borrowers to economic downturns. During business cycle booms, lenders may grow optimistic and increase credit availability as if the ideal economic and financial market conditions will persist.[3] The trade-off or costs associated with an expansion of lending is a corresponding rise in the severity of financial distress should economic conditions suddenly deteriorate. In other words, recessions that occur when individuals have more loan repayment obligations (or are more leveraged financially) are likely to be more arduous, in particular if these individuals (via job losses or pay cuts) suddenly face lower income prospects.

U.S. depository banks are required to comply with *safety and soundness* regulations, which are designed to monitor and buffer against the types of financial intermediation risks that can result in financial distress for banks and the broader economy. The propagation of intermediation risks is curbed when lending activity is restrained, but there is a cost associated with a reduction of financial risk. Recessions are likely to be milder when fewer loan repayment obligations are outstanding, but the trade-off is a less robust economic expansion. Fewer loans translate into fewer transactions that could possibly have spurred greater economic activity.[4] Consequently, determining how much financial intermediation risk is optimal for the banking system to take while simultaneously trying not to undermine economically stimulative lending activity is often a regulatory challenge.

Congressional interest in the financial conditions of depository banks, also referred to as the commercial banking system, has increased following a challenging economic and regulatory environment.[5] The conditions of the banking industry can be examined in terms of profitability, lending activity, and capitalization levels (to buffer against the financial risks); but this report focuses primarily on profitability and lending activity levels. Particular attention will be paid to metrics related to asset performance and earnings of depository banks. These measures show that profitability for the banking industry has improved, but the rate of lending activity has not returned to pre-crisis levels.

## IMPORTANT DEFINITIONS AND DISTRIBUTION BY SIZE

This report discusses the depository (commercial) banking institutions as having one aggregate balance sheet to facilitate the analysis. The following balance sheet terminology is used.

- Bank *assets* include long-term consumer, residential, and commercial loans that banks originate as well as cash and other financial securities that they hold in their asset portfolios. Bank assets will generate earnings (revenues) or losses, depending upon whether customers repay or default on their loans.
- Bank *liabilities* include the funds that they borrow. When customers (depositors) make savings or checking deposits into a bank, the bank is essentially borrowing those funds for short periods of time in order to lend them out for longer periods of time. The interest paid for these borrowings are, therefore, the costs incurred by the bank to obtain the funds necessary to originate new loans.
- Bank *capital* is the difference between the value of assets and liabilities. Bank capital includes items such as common shareholder equity, retained earnings, and provisions set aside for loan and lease losses (discussed in more detail below). Banks that accept federally insured deposits are required to maintain sufficient capital reserves to protect bank creditors from loan defaults by bank customers. Asset (loan) defaults are less likely to result in failure of a bank to repay its shorter-term obligations if sufficient capital is maintained to absorb the losses. If, however, a bank's capital falls below minimum regulatory threshold levels, it would be considered undercapitalized and faces the prospect of being shut down by its regulator, which typically appoints the Federal Deposit Insurance Company (FDIC)[6] as the receiver of the insolvent institution. Consequently, compliance with regulatory capital requirements implies that capital reserves must grow proportionately with bank asset (lending) portfolios.[7]

Assets in the banking industry are not evenly distributed, which means that banking firms are not identical and, for some metrics, must be analyzed separately to get a more accurate assessment of financial conditions. Using data from the FDIC, *Figure 1* illustrates the number of U.S. banks over time by the following size categories of bank asset holdings (defined below): less than $100 million, $100 million-$1 billion, $1 billion-$10 billion, and greater than $10 billion. Community banks are commonly defined as financial institutions with total assets below $1 billion.[8] At the other extreme are the large financial institutions that have $10 billion or more in assets. The number of banks with more than $10 billion in assets has remained relatively constant, ranging from 95 to 108 institutions over the period.

*Figure 1* also shows the dollar amount of bank assets in millions of dollars. As of 2013, the FDIC reports that industry assets were $14,722.80 billion.[9] For several decades, bank assets have increased while the number of banking institutions has declined.

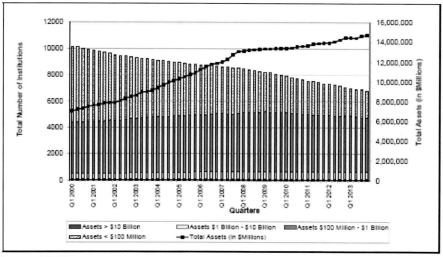

Source: FDIC.

Notes: The number of institutions holding $10 billion or more in assets appears as red dots sitting on the horizontal axis. The number of institutions range from 95 to 107 over the entire period.

Figure 1. FDIC-Insured Institutions by Asset Size and Industry Asset Holdings. (2000-2013)

The smallest of the community banks, those with less than $100 million and collectively holding approximately 1% of all industry assets, have accounted for most of the industry consolidation even prior to the 2007- 2009 recession. Banks with more than $10 billion in assets collectively hold approximately 80% of all industry assets. Consequently, profitability and lending activities may differ by bank size.

## OVERVIEW OF BANK INDUSTRY CONDITIONS

The banking system recently saw unusually high numbers of distressed institutions, with failures at rates not seen since the savings and loan crisis that began in 1980 and lasted through the early 1990s.[10] The number of banks that failed, or fell substantially below their minimum capital reserve requirements, increased as the financial crisis of 2008 unfolded. No banks failed in 2005 and 2006, and three bank failures occurred in 2007.[11] In contrast, the FDIC administered 25 bank failures in 2008, 140 bank failures in 2009, and 157 bank failures in 2010. The bank failure rate has since diminished with 92 bank failures in 2011, 51 bank failures in 2012, and 24 bank failures in 2013.[12]

Of the 6,812 FDIC-insured institutions in 2013, the FDIC reports that approximately 35% reported negative quarterly income at various quarters after the financial crisis; the percentage of these unprofitable institutions fell to 12.2% by the fourth quarter of 2013 from 15% in the fourth quarter of 2012. The FDIC also maintains a problem list of banks at risk of failure because their capital reserves have fallen below regulatory minimum levels (but perhaps not yet far enough below to be shut down). The number of depository institutions on the FDIC's problem list rose from 52 banks in 2005, peaked at **888** in the first quarter of 2011, before falling to 467 by the end of 2013.[13] *Figure 2* shows the number of FDIC-insured banks, the number of problem banks, and the number of unprofitable institutions by quarter since 2005. Note that an unprofitable institution may not be counted on the FDIC's problem institution list if it has enough capital to absorb its quarterly revenue shortfalls and still meet the *adequately capitalized* or *well-capitalized* thresholds.[14]

The industry has returned to profitability. The FDIC reports that industry full-year net income rose to $154.7 billion in 2013, representing the highest net income level since 2006.[15] Although lending growth has increased, the FDIC reports that most of the earnings increase can be attributed to increases in noninterest (fee) income and lower provisions set aside for anticipated loan losses, discussed in more detail below.

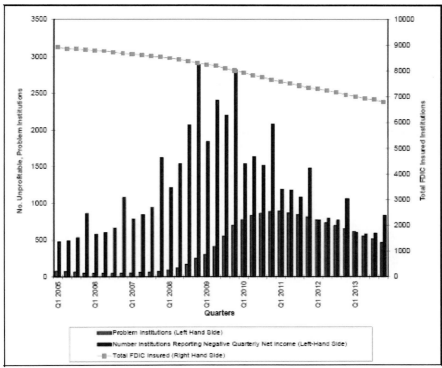

Source: FDIC.

Notes: The number of institutions reporting negative quarterly net income is computed by multiplying the total number of FDIC-insured institutions by the percentage of unprofitable institutions reported by the FDIC.

Figure 2. Total FDIC Insured, Total Problem, Total Unprofitable Institutions. (2005-2013)

Return on assets (RoA) and return on equity (RoE) are commonly used metrics to gauge bank profitability. RoA is computed with net income (total assets minus total liabilities) in the numerator and average total assets in the denominator. The RoA measures the financial return of a bank's average assets or lending activities. Given that the banking industry relies heavily upon borrowed liabilities to fund assets, the numerator of the ratio would be significantly smaller than the denominator; therefore, a RoA of approximately 1% is considered profitable.[16] RoE is computed with net income in the numerator and the total amount of common shareholder equity in the denominator. The RoE is a measure of financial return for shareholders. Unlike RoA, RoE does not have a barometer of "acceptable" performance because it can increase due to either asset profitability or depleting capital positions, making it difficult to establish a benchmark standard.[17]

The FDIC reported industry declines in both RoA and RoE during the 2007-2009 recession as the numerators of both ratios fell even faster than their denominators. The negative returns coincided with the wave of loan defaults that also occurred during the recession, which led to deterioration of capital, increases in the number of banks on the FDIC's problem list, and increases in bank failures. The RoA and RoE measures, which are illustrated in *Figure 3*, have exhibited a reversal in course since the recession.

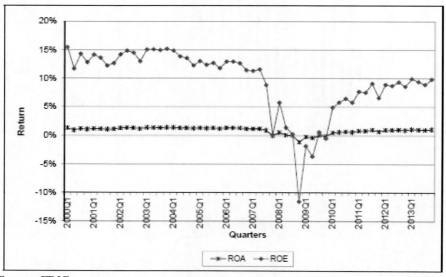

Source: FDIC.

Figure 3. Return on Assets, Return on Equity. (2000-2013)

As previously stated, declines in RoA and RoE may be attributed to loan repayment problems that led to an increase in the numbers of distressed institutions. *Non-current assets* are loans that borrowers do not repay as scheduled. The *allowances for loan and lease losses* (ALLL) is a component of regulatory bank capital set aside for anticipated (or estimated) loan losses. *Loan loss provisioning* refers to increasing the amount of ALLL when loan default risks increase; decreases are referred to as *charge-offs* or deductions from ALLL when lenders determine that non-current assets will not be repaid.[18] *Figure 4* shows the increase in both noncurrent assets and charge-offs after 2007.

Banking organizations are required to hold capital for both anticipated and unanticipated default risks. The federal bank regulators believe that most banking organizations already hold sufficient capital to meet the proposed higher requirements to buffer against *unanticipated* losses.[19] On the other hand, ALLL requirements change more frequently (quarterly) or when expected credit losses may have increased. Hence, a bank may have sufficient capital to meet unanticipated defaults, which may be associated with unforeseen events (such as a sudden increase in the unemployment rate), but it may still need to increase ALLL provisions should a borrower begin showing signs of repayment difficulties that may go into default. If banks can absorb anticipated loan losses using current income earnings, their capital will be left intact for unanticipated losses.

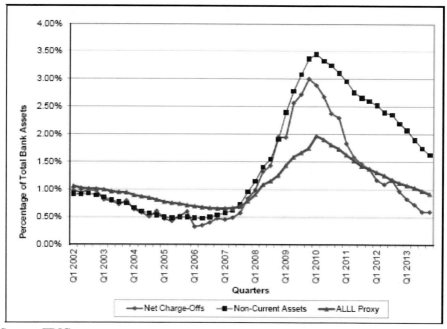

Source: FDIC.
Notes: The ALLL proxy is computed by CRS using FDIC data.

Figure 4. Non-Current Assets, Net Charge-Offs, Allowance for Loan & Lease Losses (ALLL Proxy)

The ratio of aggregate ALLL provisioning to total bank assets, also shown in *Figure 4*, is an ALLL proxy. Loan loss provisioning matched and often exceeded the *anticipated* percentage of problem assets prior to 2007, which are composed of net charge-offs and non-current assets.[20]

Despite the aggregate decline of ALLL provisioning for 15 consecutive quarters as of December 2013, the ALLL indicator suggests that the amount of loan loss provisioning after the end of 2013 appears to cover net charge-offs.[21] The percentage of non-current loans, however, must decline even more relative to the current level of ALLL provisioning (or ALLL provisioning must increase more) before the industry can fully cover its anticipated default risks.

Although the ALLL indicator in *Figure 4* was constructed for illustrative purposes, the *coverage ratio*, which is defined as the amount of loan loss reserves and equity per dollar of noncurrent loans, is more commonly used to assess the extent of non-performing assets relative to ALLL levels.[22] The more rapid pace of non-current loans led to a substantial decline in the industry coverage ratio, shown in *Figure 5*. A coverage ratio below 100% indicates that there is insufficient ALLL to cover weak loans that could go into further distress. Consequently, regulators are requiring banks to increase loan loss provisioning (as well as other components of regulatory capital) to levels that better match the levels of problem loans.[23] The FDIC reports that the coverage ratio has been rising over recent quarters as the amount of noncurrent loans has declined (relative to ALLL reserves).[24]

As regulators have taken measures to restore ALLL and other components of bank capital to higher levels, the growth rate of bank lending portfolios is likely to be affected. Similarly, a weak demand for loans or decline in the number of borrowers deemed creditworthy can also cause banks to make fewer loans, meaning that asset portfolios would grow at a slower pace.[25] The asset growth rate is computed as the percentage change in total assets from quarter to quarter, and is shown in *Figure 6*. The asset growth rate fell below negative 2% beginning in the first quarter of 2009, which had not occurred since the 1990-1991 recession[26], and remained negative until a year later; 2010 also saw negative asset growth during the second and fourth quarters. Given the magnitude of loan repayment problems, banks grew more cautious about lending (or growing their asset portfolios) to avoid the risk of further weakening their ALLL and capital reserve positions, which are more difficult to keep in regulatory compliance in a distressed environment. Consequently, although the rate of bank lending has increased since the recession and is currently positive, it has not returned to pre-recessionary levels despite the industry's return to profitability.

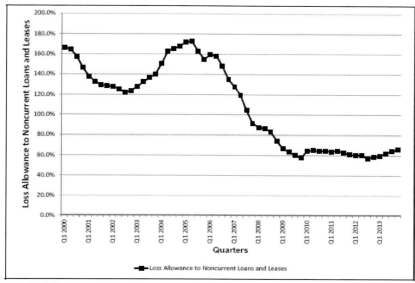

Source: FDIC.

Figure 5. Coverage Ratio. (2000-2013)

Source: FDIC.
Notes: The asset growth rate is shown as a moving average, which was computed by
CRS.

Figure 6. Asset Growth Rate. (2000-2013)

*Figure 7* illustrates some of the more common types of asset holdings in the aggregate banking portfolio. Since the 2007-2009 recession, the banking system holds larger shares of cash and smaller shares of residential mortgages, which is computed in *Figure 7* using 1-4 family residential mortgages and home equity lines of credit. From 2000 to 2013, cash holdings grew from approximately 5% to 12% of aggregate portfolio holdings. Over the same period, the share of residential mortgage credit grew from 20% to a peak of almost 24% in 2005, and this share has since steadily declined (by approximately 33%) to slightly below 16% by the end of 2013. Commercial real estate loans have declined (by approximately 20%) from its peak of almost 15% in 2007 to below 12% by the end of 2013. Hence, the amount of real estate lending in bank portfolios has declined. The total asset share represented by consumer loans (e.g., credit cards, installment loans), commercial & industrial (C&I) loans, and securities (e.g., mortgage-backed securities, state and municipal bonds, U.S. Treasury securities) have remained relatively stable over the observed 2000-2013 period.

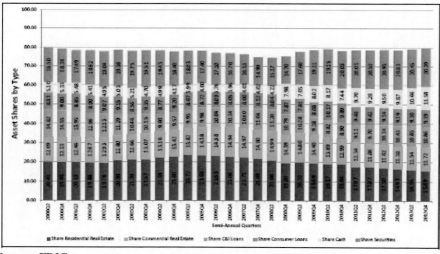

Source: FDIC.
Note: The asset shares are computed by CRS using FDIC data.

Figure 7. Composition of Assets. (2000-2013)

## OVERVIEW OF REVENUE COMPOSITION BY BANK SIZE

As previously stated, banks typically borrow funds from depositors for shorter periods of time relative to their originated loans. Banks must continuously renew their short-term borrowings until longer-term loans have been fully repaid. For example, suppose a bank originates a consumer loan that is expected to be repaid in full over two years. Over the two years that the loan is being repaid, the bank will simultaneously "fund the loan," meaning that it will treat its depositors' funds as a sequence of quarterly (for a total of eight quarters) or monthly (for a total of 24 months) short-term loans and make periodic interest payments to depositors.[27] The spread or difference between lending long and borrowing short is known as the *net interest margin*.

Smaller banks typically engage in "relationship banking," meaning that they develop close familiarity with their respective customer bases and typically provide financial services within a circumscribed geographical area. Relationship banking allows these institutions to capture lending risks that are unique, infrequent, and localized. These institutions, which rely heavily on commercial (real estate and retail) lending and funding with deposits, typically have higher net interest margins than large banks. Funding loans with deposits is cheaper than accessing the short-term financial markets, particularly for small institutions that do not have the transaction volume or size to justify the higher costs.

In contrast, large institutions typically engage in "transactional banking" or high-volume lending that employs automated underwriting methodologies that often cannot capture atypical lending risks.[28] Large banks are not as dependent upon deposits to fund their lending activities given their greater ability to access short-term money markets. Large banks typically have lower spreads because their large-scale activities generate large amounts of fee income from a wide range of activities, which can be used to cover the costs of borrowing in the short-term money markets.[29] Revenues are earned by originating and selling large amounts of loans to nonbank institutions, such as government-sponsored enterprises (Fannie Mae and Freddie Mac) and non-depository institutions that hold financial assets (e.g., insurance companies, hedge funds). A large share of fees are still generated from traditional banking activities (e.g., safe deposit, payroll processing, trust services, payment services) and from facilitating daily purchase and payment transactions, in which service fees may be collected from checking, money orders, and electronic payment card (debit and credit) transactions.[30] Hence, transactional or high-volume banking activities allow large banks to generate fee income and engage in financial transactions characterized by minimum deal size or institutional size requirements, which simultaneously act as a barrier to participation by community banks.[31]

Given the differences in the composition of bank revenue streams, the net interest margins and fee income streams are illustrated by asset size categories. *Figure 8* presents the net interest margins (or spreads) by bank size. By 2009, the net interest margins had declined for small banks, but they still remained higher over time than the margins for larger banks. The net interest margins for large banks increased over the recession period as they experienced a large influx of deposits during the recession, perhaps due to uncertainty in the money market; this "flight to safety" influx resulted in a substantial drop in their funding costs.[32] In other words, large banks were able to rely relatively less on short-term financial markets and could, instead, take advantage of cheaper funding from deposits. Although net interest margins may appear to be returning to pre-recession trends, the future performance of this spread would still be affected by a shift in the composition of asset holdings.

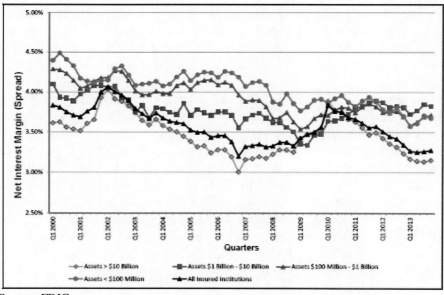

Source: FDIC.

Figure 8. Net Interest Margins by Bank Size Categories. (2000-2013)

For example, the spread may be affected by an increase in liquid asset holdings (e.g., securities backed by the U.S. federal government), perhaps due to weaker demand for more illiquid loans (e.g., mortgages, commercial loans) or lower capital requirements associated with holding more liquid loans. Banks may alter the composition of their asset portfolios, attempting to seek higher yielding lending opportunities (e.g., holding less mortgages and more credit card loans) to help maintain spreads above 3%. Bank spreads may also be affected by the amount of deposits that remain or flow out of the banking system as the economy strengthens. Hence, it has become more challenging to predict future profitability arising from more traditional lending activities.

*Figure 9* presents non-interest income as a percentage of assets by bank size. The overall profitability trend of fee generating activities has rebounded since the recession, but there appears to be more volatility in the fee income revenues of smaller institutions. Although greater reliance upon fee income as a percentage of (large) bank income suggests a reduction in exposure to credit and funding risks, it may not necessarily translate into greater stability of earnings streams.[33]

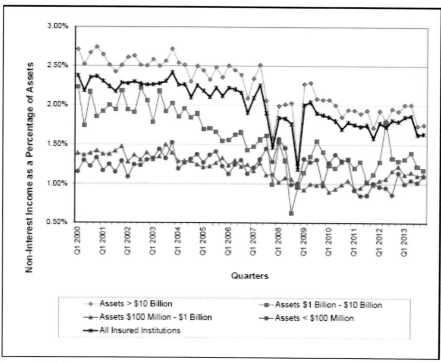

Source: FDIC.

Figure 9. Percentage of Non-Interest Income by Bank Size Categories. (2000-2013)

For example, banks no longer generate as much fee income by selling (mortgage) loans to the private-label securitization markets, particularly those largely abandoned by investors at the beginning of the financial crisis.[34] In other words, high-volume fee-generating transactions are still dependent upon fluctuations in investor demand for securities that are created from securitized (structured finance) deals, which adds variability to income. In addition, regulatory costs may reduce fee income. Recent regulation of credit card fees as well as on fees that large institutions may collect from debit transactions would affect the earnings streams.[35] Banks would likely seek new opportunities to provide financial services to generate new fee revenues.[36] Hence, future fee generating activities are still affected by financial market uncertainty.

## CONCLUSION

The banking industry has exhibited profitability since the 2007-2009 financial crisis. Net interest margins and fee income as a percentage of assets are less volatile now than when the U.S. economy was in recession. The industry, however, still has more non-current assets than allowances for loan and lease losses; and there are still hundreds of banks on the FDIC's problem list. These factors may be influencing the asset growth rate, which has been positive since 2011, but remains below the average rate of growth observed over the past two decades.

Profitability in the banking industry should not be interpreted as evidence of a return to previous lending patterns given that the industry is adapting its business model under the new regulatory environment. Lending costs are expected to increase for depository banks as a result of higher overall capital requirements established by the Basel Committee on Banking Supervision and by the Dodd-Frank Wall Street Reform and Consumer Protection Act of 2010 (P.L. 111-203, 124 Stat. 1376).[37] Given that large banks are less dependent upon traditional lending activities than smaller banks, the large institutions may be able to generate enough fee income from a wide range of other financial activities to remain profitable even if lending activity does not resemble pre-recessionary levels. Hence, profitability trends may differ for banks by size.

# End Notes

[1] Underwriting in banking refers to two types of activities. Loan underwriting occurs when a bank performs a (default) risk assessment of a potential borrower to determine whether to extend credit (loanable funds), the amount, and how much to charge the borrower. Securities underwriting occurs when a bank agrees to take on the risk of distributing securities (in the form of bonds or stocks) of another entity that wishes to attract outside investors to provide funding. If, however, the bank is unable to find enough interested investors, then it retains any unsold securities and assumes the default risk associated with the entity. The Glass-Steagall Act restricts the securities underwriting activities of depository banks. Depository banks may underwrite federal, state, and local government securities as well as the securities guaranteed by federal or state governments; but they are not allowed to underwrite equity securities (corporate stock). See CRS Report R41181, Permissible Securities Activities of Commercial Banks Under the Glass-Steagall Act (GSA) and the Gramm-Leach-Bliley Act (GLBA), by David H. Carpenter and M. Maureen Murphy.

[2] This phenomenon is known as a bank run. The federal deposit insurance system in the United States was established in the1930s to insure deposits, which helps to sustain public confidence and avoid runs on U.S. banks. See CRS Report R41718, Federal Deposit Insurance for Banks and Credit Unions, by Darryl E. Getter.

[3] See Hyman P. Minsky, The Financial Instability Hypothesis, The Jerome Levy Economics Institute, Working Paper no. 74, May 1992.

[4] Bank capital levels may become less effective at reducing intermediation risks if lending activities migrate outside of the regulated banking system and are conducted by institutions that do not hold federally insured deposits.

[5] For a summary of some challenges facing financial institutions, see CRS Report R43364, Recent Trends in Consumer Retail Payment Services Delivered by Depository Institutions, by Darryl E. Getter.

[6] When a bank fails, the Federal Deposit Insurance Corporation (FDIC) typically closes the institution and administers the repayment of depositors. See CRS Report R41718, Federal Deposit Insurance for Banks and Credit Unions, by Darryl E. Getter.

[7] Regulators require banks to maintain minimum capital-asset ratio levels, thus maintaining the proportional growth of assets and capital. Capital-asset ratios are computed by placing a financial institution's total capital in the numerator of the ratio and then dividing by its total assets, which are usually weighted by degree of default risk. Note that this analysis will focus primarily on the component of capital most closely associated with loan losses rather than discuss the more complex aspects of capital regulation. See Douglas J. Elliot, "A Primer on Bank Capital," The Brookings Institution, January 28, 2010, at http://www.brookings.edu/~/media/research/files/papers/2010/1/29%20capital%20elliott/0129_capital_primer_elliott.pdf; and CRS Report R42744, U.S. Implementation of the Basel Capital Regulatory Framework, by Darryl E. Getter.

[8] An alternate and more extensive definition of a community bank is associated with its functions as opposed to its asset size. See Federal Deposit Insurance Corporation, FDIC Community Banking Study, Washington, DC, December 2012, at http://www.fdic.gov/ regulations /resources/cbi/report/cbi-full.pdf.

[9] See FDIC Quarterly Banking Report as of December 31, 2013, at http://www2.fdic.gov/ qbp/ 2013dec/qbp.pdf.

[10] See Federal Deposit Insurance Corporation, Division of Research and Statistics, Chapter 4: The Savings and Loan Crisis and Its Relationship to Banking, History of the Eighties— Lessons for the Future: An Examination of the Banking Crises of the 1980s and Early 1990s, Washington, DC, at http://www.fdic.gov/bank/historical/history/ 167_188.pdf.

[11] See FDIC Quarterly Banking Report as of December 31, 2009, at http://www2.fdic.gov/qbp/2009dec/qbp.pdf.

[12] See FDIC Quarterly Banking Report as of December 31, 2013, at http://www2.fdic.gov/qbp/2013dec/qbp.pdf.

[13] Given that the assets of the problem institutions represent approximately 1.04% of total industry assets, the remaining distressed institutions are likely to be small.

[14] The italicized terms refer to the capitalization categories established under the Prompt Corrective Action system of bank regulatory rules, which may be found at http://www.fdic.gov/regulations/laws/rules/2000-4400.html.

[15] See FDIC, "FDIC-Insured Institutions Earned $40.3 Billion in the Fourth Quarter of 2013," press release, February 26, 2014, http://www.fdic.gov/news/news/press/2014/pr14012.html.

[16] See Ricki Helfner, chairman, "On the Release of the Quarterly Banking Profile," Speech at Federal Deposit Insurance Corporation, Washington, DC, September 12, 1995, at http://www.fdic.gov/news/news/speeches/archives/ 1995/sp12sept95.html.

[17] See European Central Bank, Beyond RoE—How to Measure Bank Performance, Appendix to the Report on EU Banking Structures, Germany, September 2010, http://www.ecb.europa.eu/pub/pdf/other/ beyondroehowtomeasurebankperformance201009en.pdf.

[18] Net charge-offs are charge-offs minus the delinquent loans that recover. Mortgage and credit card charge-offs differ. A credit card loan charge-off can be recognized immediately, but writing off mortgages takes considerably more time. When it becomes clear that a mortgage default cannot be cured, the property is generally seized via foreclosure and must be resold to recover some losses. For more information on the foreclosure process, see Appendix A of CRS Report R41572, Incentives and Factors Influencing Foreclosure and Other Loss Mitigation Outcomes, by Darryl E. Getter.

[19] See Department of the Treasury: Office of the Comptroller of the Currency, Federal Reserve System, Federal Deposit Insurance Corporation, "Regulatory Capital Rules: Regulatory Capital, Implementation of Basel III, Minimum Regulatory Capital Ratios, Capital Adequacy, Transition Provisions, and Prompt Corrective Action," 77 Federal Register 52796, August 30, 2012 at http://www.gpo.gov/fdsys/pkg/FR-2012-08-30/pdf/2012-16757.pdf; and U.S. Congress, Senate Committee on Banking, Housing, and Urban Affairs, Basel III, Testimony of Michael S. Gibson, Director, Division of Banking Supervision and Regulation, Federal Reserve Board, 112th Cong., 2nd sess., November 14, 2012, at http://www.federalreserve.gov/newsevents/testimony/gibson20121114a.htm.

[20] The ratio of ALLL-to-total assets in this analysis follows a similar practice found in Luc Laeven and Giovanni Majnoni, "Loan Loss Provisioning and Economic Slowdowns: Too Much, Too Late?" Journal of Financial Intermediation, vol. 12, no. 2 (April 2003), pp. 178-197. Loan loss reserve proceeds, however, must come from current income earnings as opposed to total assets.

[21] For more details on the decline in loan loss provisions, see FDIC Quarterly Banking Reports for March 31, 2012, at http://www2.fdic.gov/qbp/2012mar/qbp.pdf and December 31, 2013, at http://www2.fdic.gov/qbp/2013dec/qbp.pdf.

[22] See James B. Thomson, "Current Banking Conditions, FDIC-Insured Institutions," Federal Reserve Bank of Cleveland, Economic Trends, June 1, 2010, at http://www.clevelandfed.org/research/trends/2010/0610/02banfin.cfm.

[23] In addition to responding to higher balance sheet risks, regulators are implementing Basel II.5, Basel III, and the Dodd-Frank Wall Street Reform and Consumer Protection Act of 2010 (Dodd-Frank Act; P.L. 111-203), which collectively will result in higher bank capital requirements. See CRS Report R42744, U.S. Implementation of the Basel Capital Regulatory Framework, by Darryl E. Getter.

[24] See FDIC Quarterly Banking Report as of December 31, 2013, p. 2, at http://www2.fdic.gov/qbp/2013dec/qbp.pdf.

[25] See CRS Report R41623, U.S. Household Debt Reduction, by Darryl E. Getter.

[26] See National Bureau of Economic Research Business Cycle Dating Committee, March 1991, at http://www.nber.org/ March91.html.

[27] For example, if a bank originates a two-year loan at a fixed 6% interest rate and pays depositors a 2% return, then the net interest margin or spread would be 4%. Given that the 6% rate is fixed, fluctuations in short-term interest rates mean that the spread would also fluctuate over the two years that the loan is being repaid.

[28] For more information on automated underwriting, see Wayne Passmore and Roger Sparks, The Effect of Automated Underwriting on the Profitability of Mortgage Securitization, Federal Reserve Board, Finance and Discussion Series 1997-19, Washington, DC, 1997, at http://www.federalreserve.gov/pubs/feds/1997/199719/199719abs.html.

[29] See Judy Plock, Mike Anas, and David Van Vickle, "Does Net Interest Margin Matter to Banks?," Federal Deposit Insurance Corporation, FDIC Outlook, June 2, 2004, at http://www.fdic.gov/bank/analytical/regional/ro20042q/na/ infocus.html.

[30] See CRS Report R41529, Supervision of U.S. Payment, Clearing, and Settlement Systems: Designation of Financial Market Utilities (FMUs), by Marc Labonte.

[31] See Conference of State Bank Supervisors, Community Banks and Capital: Assessing a Community Bank's Need and Access to Capital in the Face of Market and Regulatory Challenges, December 2011, at http://CSBSCommunityBanksCapital White Paper120 811.pdf.

[32] For more information on the influx of deposits into the banking system, see Paul Davis, "In Cash Glut, Banks Try to Discourage New Deposits," American Banker, July 2010, at http://www.americanbanker.com/bulletins/-1023018- 1.html; Office of the Comptroller of the Currency, Semi-Annual Risk Perspective, Spring 2012, at http://occ.gov/ publications/publications-by-type/other-publications-reports/semiannual-risk-perspective/semiannual-risk-perspectivespring-2012.pdf. Many depositors may have moved money to larger banks in response to uncertainty in the money markets. For discussions about money market funds falling below $1 per share, see Nada Mora, "Can Banks Provide Liquidity in a Financial Crisis?," Economic Review, Federal Reserve Bank of Kansas City, Third Quarter 2010, pp. 31- 68; CRS Report R42083, Financial Stability Oversight Council: A Framework to Mitigate Systemic Risk, by Edward V. Murphy; and CRS Report R42787, An Overview of the Transaction Account Guarantee (TAG) Program and the Potential Impact of Its Expiration or Extension, by Sean M. Hoskins.

[33] Robert DeYoung and Tara Rice, "How Do Banks Make Money? The Fallacies of Fee Income," Federal Reserve Bank of Chicago, Economic Perspectives, 2004, pp. 34-51, at http://www.chicagofed.org/digital_assets/publications/ economic_perspectives/2004/ep_4qtr2004_part3_DeYoung_Rice.pdf.

[34] For information on securitization markets issues, see U.S. Congress, Senate Committee on Banking, Housing, and Urban Affairs, Subcommittee on Securities, Insurance and Investment, Securitization of Assets: Problems and Solutions, Testimony of George P. Miller, American Securitization Forum, 111th Cong., 1st sess., October 7, 2009.

[35] See CRS Report RL34393, The Credit Card Market: Recent Trends and Regulatory Actions, by Darryl E. Getter; and CRS Report R41913, Regulation of Debit Interchange Fees, by Darryl E. Getter.

[36] See CRS Report R43364, Recent Trends in Consumer Retail Payment Services Delivered by Depository Institutions, by Darryl E. Getter.

[37] For more information on the Basel Committee of Banking Supervisors and the Basel III Accord, see http://www.bis.org/.

In: Money, Economics, and Finance. Volume 3    ISBN: 978-1-63321-505-4
Editor: Clifford Dobrowski                © 2014 Nova Science Publishers, Inc.

*Chapter 5*

# GOVERNMENT ASSISTANCE FOR AIG: SUMMARY AND COST[*]

## *Baird Webel*

## SUMMARY

American International Group (AIG), one of the world's major insurers, was the largest direct recipient of government financial assistance during the recent financial crisis. At the maximum, the Federal Reserve (Fed) and the Treasury committed approximately $182.3 billion in specific extraordinary assistance for AIG and another $15.9 billion through a more widely available lending facility. The amount actually disbursed to assist AIG reached a maximum of $184.6 billion in April 2009. In return, AIG paid interest and dividends on the funding and the U.S. Treasury ultimately received a 92% ownership share in the company. As of December 14, 2012, the government assistance for AIG ended. All Federal Reserve loans have been repaid and the Treasury has sold all of the common equity that resulted from the assistance.

Going into the financial crisis, the overarching AIG holding company was regulated by the Office of Thrift Supervision (OTS), but most of its U.S. operating subsidiaries were regulated by various states. Because AIG was primarily an insurer, it was largely outside of the normal Federal Reserve facilities that lend to thrifts facing liquidity

---

[*] This is an edited, reformatted and augmented version of a Congressional Research Service publication R42953, prepared for Members and Committees of Congress, dated August 14, 2013.

difficulties and it was also outside of the normal Federal Deposit Insurance Corporation (FDIC) receivership provisions that apply to banking institutions. September 2008 saw a panic in financial markets marked by the failure of large financial institutions, such as Fannie Mae, Freddie Mac, and Lehman Brothers. In addition to suffering from the general market downturn, AIG faced extraordinary losses resulting largely from two sources: (1) the AIG Financial Products subsidiary, which specialized in financial derivatives and was primarily the regulatory responsibility of the OTS; and (2) a securities lending program, which used securities originating in the state-regulated insurance subsidiaries. In the panic conditions prevailing at the time, the Federal Reserve determined that "a disorderly failure of AIG could add to already significant levels of financial market fragility" and stepped in to support the company. Had AIG not been given assistance by the government, bankruptcy seemed a near certainty. The Federal Reserve support was later supplemented and ultimately replaced by assistance from the U.S. Treasury's Troubled Asset Relief Program (TARP).

The AIG rescue produced unexpected financial returns for the government. The Fed loans were completely repaid and it directly received $18.1 billion in interest, dividends, and capital gains. In addition, another $17.5 billion in capital gains from the Fed assistance accrued to the Treasury. The $67.8 billion in TARP assistance, however, resulted in a negative return to the government, as only $54.4 billion was recouped from asset sales and $0.9 billion was received in dividend payments. If one offsets the negative return to TARP of $12.5 billion with the $35.6 billion in positive returns for the Fed assistance, the entire assistance for AIG showed a positive return of approximately $23.1 billion. It should be noted that these figures are the simple cash returns from the AIG transactions and do not take into account the full economic costs of the assistance. Fully accounting for these costs would result in lower returns to the government, although no agency has performed such a full assessment of the AIG assistance. The latest Congressional Budget Office (CBO) estimate of the budgetary cost of the TARP assistance for AIG, which is a broader economic analysis of the cost, found a loss of $15 billion compared with the $12.5 billion cash loss. CBO does not, however, regularly perform cost estimates on Federal Reserve actions.

Congressional interest in the AIG intervention relates to oversight of the Federal Reserve and TARP, as well as general policy measures to promote financial stability. Specific attention has focused on perceived corporate profligacy, particularly compensation for AIG employees, which was the subject of a hearing in the 113th Congress and legislation in the 111th Congress.

# INTRODUCTION

In 2007, American International Group (AIG) was the fifth-largest insurer in the world with $110 billion in overall revenues. In the United States, it ranked second in property/casualty insurance premiums ($37.7 billion/7.5% market share) and first in life insurance premiums ($53.0 billion/8.9%). For particular lines, AIG ranked first in surplus lines, ninth in private passenger auto, first in overall commercial lines (fifth in commercial auto), and fourth in mortgage guaranty. It was outside the top 10 in homeowners insurance.[1] According to the National Association of Insurance Commissioners (NAIC), AIG had more than 70 state-regulated insurance subsidiaries in the United States, with more than 175 non-insurance or foreign entities under the general holding company.

Although primarily operating as an insurer, prior to the crisis AIG was overseen at the holding company level by the federal Office of Thrift Supervision (OTS) because the company owned a relatively small thrift subsidiary. The bulk of the company's insurance operations were regulated by the individual state regulators as, per the 1945 McCarran-Ferguson Act,[2] the states act as the primary regulators of the business of insurance. Because AIG was primarily an insurer, it was largely outside of the normal Federal Reserve (Fed) facilities that lend to thrifts (and banks) facing liquidity difficulties and it was also outside of the normal Federal Deposit Insurance Corporation (FDIC) receivership provisions that apply to FDIC-insured depository institutions.

AIG, as did most financial institutions, suffered losses on a wide variety of financial instruments in 2008. The exceptional losses which resulted in the essential failure of AIG arose primarily from two sources: the derivative activities of the AIG Financial Products (AIGFP) subsidiary and the securities lending activities managed by AIG Investments with securities largely from the AIG insurance subsidiaries. Regulatory oversight of these sources was split. The OTS was responsible for oversight of AIGFP, while the state insurance regulators were responsible for oversight of the insurance subsidiaries which supplied the securities lending operations, and would ultimately bear losses if the securities, or their equivalent value, could not be returned.

With the company facing losses on various operations, AIG experienced a significant decline in its stock price and downgrades from the major credit rating agencies in 2008.[3] These downgrades led to immediate demands for significant amounts of collateral (approximately $14 billion to $15 billion in collateral payments, according to contemporary press reports).[4] As financial demands on the company mounted, bankruptcy appeared a possibility, as occurred with Lehman Brothers in the same timeframe. Fears about the spillover effects from such a failure brought calls for government action to avert such a failure. Many feared that AIG was "too big to fail"[5] due to the potential for widespread disruption to financial markets resulting from such a failure. AIG's size was not the only concern in this regard, but also its innumerable connections to other financial institutions.

The New York Insurance Superintendent, primary regulator of many of the AIG insurance subsidiaries, led an effort to provide the parent AIG holding company with access to up to $20 billion in cash from AIG's insurance subsidiaries, which were perceived as solvent and relatively liquid. Ultimately, this transfer did not take place and efforts to find private funding for AIG failed as well; instead, the Federal Reserve approved an extraordinary loan of up to $85 billion in September 2008. As AIG's financial position weakened following the initial Fed loan, several rounds of additional funding were provided to AIG by both the Fed and the Treasury's Troubled Asset Relief Program (TARP). Assistance to AIG was restructured several times, including loosening of the terms of the assistance[6] (see *Appendix A* below for more complete discussion of the changes to AIG's assistance).

The 2010 Dodd-Frank Act[7] overhauled the financial regulatory structure in the United States. Of particular note with regard to AIG, the act moved all federal financial holding company regulation to the Federal Reserve and moved the oversight of thrift subsidiaries to the Office of the Comptroller of the Currency. Thus, both the AIG holding company and the AIG thrift subsidiary are currently overseen by different agencies than before the crisis.[8] In addition, the act created a Financial Stability Oversight Council (FSOC) and the possibility of enhanced regulation by the Fed of institutions deemed systemically important. AIG was designated as systemically significant in July 2013, and will thus be subject to Fed oversight going forward.[9] The act also put restrictions on the Federal Reserve's lending authority that would limit its ability to make future extraordinary assistance available to individual companies, as was done in the case of AIG. The Dodd-Frank Act did not create a federal insurance regulator; thus the states continue to be the primary regulators of the various insurance operations of AIG.

The assistance for AIG has provoked controversy on several different levels. Significant attention, and anger, has been directed at questions of employee compensation. Following reports of bonuses being paid for employees of AIGFP, the House passed legislation (H.R. 1664, 111th Congress) aimed at prohibiting "unreasonable and excessive compensation and compensation not based on performance standards" for TARP recipients, including AIG (see *Appendix B* for additional information on executive compensation restrictions under TARP). Issues around TARP compensation continue in the 113th Congress, with the House Committee on Oversight & Government Reform's Subcommittee on Economic Growth, Job Creation & Regulatory Affairs holding a hearing entitled "Bailout Rewards: The Treasury Department's Continued Approval of Excessive Pay for Executives at Taxpayer-Funded Companies" on February 26, 2013.[10]

Questions have also been raised about the transparency and legality of the assistance. Although the billions of dollars in government assistance went to the AIG, in many cases, it can be argued that AIG has acted as an intermediary for this assistance. In short order after drawing on government assistance, substantial funds flowed out of AIG to entities on the other side of AIG's financial transactions, such as securities lending or credit default swaps. Seen from this view, the true beneficiary of many of the federal funds that flowed to AIG was not AIG itself, but instead AIG's counterparties, who may not have received full payment in the event of a bankruptcy. In the interest of transparency, many argued that AIG's counterparties, particularly those who received payments facilitated by government assistance, should be identified. Many of these counterparties were only identified after public and congressional pressure.[11]

Lawsuits challenging the legality of the government actions relating to the assistance, particularly the equity taken as part of this assistance, have been filed by Starr International Company, Inc. (Starr). This company is owned by Maurice "Hank" Greenberg, formerly the CEO of AIG and a major stockholder in the company. Starr has sought compensation for the allegedly unconstitutional taking of AIG shareholder property without compensation in connection with the federal assistance package rescuing AIG from bankruptcy. The Board of Directors of AIG declined to join this suit in January 2013, but it is still pending before the Court of Federal Claims.[12]

## SUMMARY OF GOVERNMENT ASSISTANCE TO AIG

The extraordinary direct government assistance for AIG that began in September 2008 has ended. All loans to assist AIG have been repaid and the assets purchased from AIG by Federal Reserve entities have been sold. The common equity holdings in AIG that resulted from both Federal Reserve and U.S. Treasury TARP assistance for AIG have been sold. The final connection between the government and AIG was a relatively small amount of warrants issued to the Treasury as part of the TARP assistance. AIG repurchased these warrants for approximately $25 million on March 1, 2013.[13] With the sale of the TARP equity, the TARP corporate governance and executive compensation restrictions imposed on AIG were lifted.

The government assistance for AIG took a variety of different forms, with the initial Federal Reserve loans followed by TARP assistance in three major restructurings in November 2008, March 2009, and September 2010. The following briefly summarizes the primary types of assistance (see *Appendix A* for more complete details).

## Federal Reserve Loans to AIG

The initial assistance for AIG came in the form of an $85 billion loan commitment announced on September 16, 2008. In addition to a high, variable interest rate,[14] the government received a nearly 80% share of the common equity in AIG. This loan was augmented by an additional $37.8 billion loan commitment in October 2008, which was collateralized by securities from the AIG securities lending program. The maximum amount outstanding under these loans was over $90 billion in October 2008. The limit on the Fed loan was reduced to $60 billion in November 2008 and $35 billion in March 2009. The 2009 reduction occurred as the Fed accepted $25 billion in AIG subsidiary equity as partial repayment of the loans. The loans were eventually repaid in January 2011, primarily through cash gained by AIG from sales of various assets and from TARP assistance. The Fed received a total of $8.2 billion in interest and dividends from these loans and the common equity stake resulting from the loans was sold by the Treasury for $17.5 billion. Federal Reserve profits are mostly remitted to the Treasury and such remittances more than doubled from 2007 to 2010.[15]

## Federal Reserve Loans to Finance Asset Purchases from AIG

In November 2008, the Fed loan to AIG was partially replaced by Fed loans to Limited Liability Corporations (LLCs) created and controlled by the Fed, which were known as Maiden Lane II and Maiden Lane III.[16] Up to $52.5 billion in loans from the Fed were committed to Maiden Lanes II and III with $43.8 billion actually disbursed.[17] These LLCs purchased various securities, which were an ongoing financial drain on AIG at the time. After purchase, these securities were held by the LLCs and then sold as market conditions improved. All the loans were repaid by June 2012, and the facilities ultimately returned an additional $9.5 billion in interest and other gains to the Fed.

## AIG Commercial Paper Funding Facility Borrowing

The Commercial Paper Funding Facility (CPFF) was created by the Federal Reserve in 2008 as a widely available vehicle to provide liquidity during the financial crisis.[18] AIG and its subsidiaries were approved to borrow up to a maximum of $20.9 billion, with actual borrowing reaching $16.1 billion in January 2009. AIG's CPFF borrowing is typically not included in the reporting of AIG assistance done by the Fed and Treasury. This borrowing, however, occurred at the same time as AIG was accessing the other Fed loans and TARP assistance and likely was preferred over these sources because CPFF charged lower interest rates[19] and individual CPFF borrowers and borrowing amounts were not reported by the Fed at the time. The Dodd-Frank Act required the Fed to report full details of the CPFF and other Fed facilities.[20] This reporting shows AIG borrowing beginning in October 2008 and extending until April 2010. Although interest amounts were not reported, according to CRS estimates based on the principal amounts and interest rates that were reported, the Fed appears to have received approximately $0.4 billion in interest from AIG's CPFF borrowing.

## TARP Assistance for AIG

In November 2008, $40 billion in TARP assistance was committed to AIG, and it was disbursed through Treasury purchase of AIG preferred equity.[21] The commitment was increased to nearly $70 billion in March 2009, and the maximum level of disbursement of $67.8 billion was reached in January 2011, primarily to facilitate the withdrawal of Federal Reserve involvement with AIG.[22] Although TARP assistance took the form of preferred equity purchases, $47.5 billion in AIG preferred equity was converted into common equity, which brought the government ownership stake in AIG to a high of 92% in January 2011. The Treasury began selling the common equity in May 2011 and completed the sales in December 2012. In addition to the equity, the Treasury received a relatively small number of stock warrants through TARP, which it sold back to AIG in March 2013.[23] The Treasury received $34.1 billion from its sales of the TARP common equity and approximately $25 million from the warrant sales. AIG completely redeemed the $20.3 billion in unconverted preferred equity in March 2012, and the company paid a total $0.9 billion in cash dividends to the government on this equity. Comparing the total amount disbursed to the total amount recouped shows a $12.5 billion shortfall on the TARP portion of the assistance for AIG.

*Table 1* below summarizes the direct government assistance for AIG, including maximum amounts committed by the government, the amounts actually disbursed, and the returns from this assistance.

## Indirect Assistance for AIG

Although the loans and preferred equity purchase directly aided AIG, the company also benefited from other actions taken by the U.S. government to address the financial crisis. For example, TARP provided nearly $205 billion in additional capital to U.S. banks in 2008 and early 2009. To the extent that AIG had assets that depended on the health of these banks, or liabilities, such as CDS, that might have increased with the failure of these banks, the TARP assistance for banks would have aided AIG's financial position as well as the financial position of most other financial institutions. If AIG was perceived as being "too big to fail" due to the government assistance, the company may also have received an advantage in insurance markets and in debt markets compared to other firms competing with AIG. The reputational effect of government-backing, however, also had negative effects on the company to the degree that AIG even changed the name of its primary insurance subsidiary. Such second-order effects from the government actions are difficult to quantify and typically are not included in assessments of the assistance for AIG.

Another indirect, but more definite, benefit to AIG from government action during the crisis came from policy rulings by the Internal Revenue Service (IRS).[24] Under normal circumstances, a corporation undergoing a change in control is not able to carry forward previous tax losses.[25] Government holdings gained through TARP, however, generally have not been treated by the IRS as causing such a change in control. AIG was able to report a $17.7 billion accounting gain from these tax benefits in 2011.[26] Economic theory would suggest that these tax benefits resulted in the government receiving a higher price for the AIG shares when they were sold, so the final result may not have been to increase the overall cost of the AIG assistance. Whether or not one includes these tax rulings as specific assistance for AIG, however, would significantly change the assessment of the overall financial results from the assistance. Neither the Treasury nor CBO have included these tax rulings in their assessments of the assistance for AIG.

## WHAT DID THE ASSISTANCE FOR AIG COST?

From the above accounting, which largely follows that offered by the Treasury in its announcements,[27] the cost of the AIG assistance seems relatively straightforward. Summing the various amounts of interest, dividends, and equity sales, one arrives at a total of $207.7 billion returned to the Treasury and Federal Reserve compared with a total maximum disbursement of $184.1 billion, for a positive return of $23.1 billion. This cash accounting, however, falls short of a full economic assessment of the assistance for AIG. Such assessments typically include other factors, such as the time value of money (a dollar in 2008 was not worth the same as a dollar in 2012) and the opportunity cost of the funds involved (what would the returns have been if the money involved had been used for other purposes?).

The budgetary cost estimates undertaken by the Congressional Budget Office (CBO) incorporate some broader economic principles in assessing the costs of government actions. In particular, CBO's official budgetary cost estimates for TARP must follow not only the Federal Credit Reform Act,[28] which requires that the present value of the full long-term cost of loans and loan guarantees be recognized, but also that market rates be used in these calculations rather than the lower Treasury borrowing costs.[29] These requirements have the effect of lowering the returns. This effect can be seen by comparing the CBO estimates with the more simple cash accounting above. The latest CBO estimates, which occurred after most of the AIG equity had been sold, saw a budgetary cost of $15 billion attributed to the TARP portion of the AIG assistance,[30] compared to a negative return of $12.5 billion using the simple cash accounting.

The Federal Reserve actions which make up a majority of the returns from the government assistance for AIG are not subject to regular CBO or OMB budgetary cost assessment. CBO did publish a study of the budgetary impact and subsidy cost of the Federal Reserve's response to the financial crisis in May 2010. CBO estimated a cost of $2 billion from the Federal Reserve loans to AIG at their inception,[31] compared to a final positive return of $35.6 billion on a cash accounting basis. The CBO estimates for TARP have become significantly more positive over time, and it is quite possible that, were CBO to redo the estimates at the current date, the estimate for the Federal Reserve actions would become more positive as well.

### Table 1. Summary of Direct AIG Assistance

| Type of Assistance | Maximum Amount Committed | Maximum Amount Actually Disbursed | Date of Repayment | Gain or Loss (-) on Assistance |
|---|---|---|---|---|
| Extraordinary Fed Loans to AIG | $122.8 billion (Oct. 2008) | $90.3 billion (Oct. 22, 2008) | Jan. 2011 | $25.7 billion |
| Fed Loans for Asset Purchases | $52.5 billion (Nov. 2008) | $43.8 billion (Dec. 2008) | June 2012 | $9.5 billion |
| Fed Loans through CPFF | $20.9 billion (Nov. 2008) | $16.1 billion (Jan. 2009) | April 2010 | $0.4 billion |
| TARP Preferred Share Purchases | $69.8 billion (March 2009) | $67.8 billion (Jan. 2011) | Dec. 2012 | -$12.5 billion |
| Totals | $198.2 billion (March 2009) | $184.6 billion (April 2009) | Dec. 2012 | $23.1 billion |

Source: Federal Reserve weekly H.4.1 statistical release; Federal Reserve Board and Federal Reserve Bank of NY data releases; U.S. Treasury TARP Monthly Reports; CRS calculations.

Note: Warrants associated with TARP preferred shares repurchased by AIG in March 2013. The approximately $25 million gain from this is included in the -$12.5 billion loss from the TARP shares.

# APPENDIX A. DETAILS OF GOVERNMENT ASSISTANCE FOR AIG

## Assistance Prior to TARP Involvement

### *Initial Loan*

On September 16, 2008, the Fed announced, after consultation with the Treasury Department, that it would lend up to $85 billion to AIG over the next two years. Drawing from the loan facility would only occur at the discretion of the Fed. A new CEO was installed after the initial intervention and Fed staff was put on site with the company to oversee operations. The interest rate on the funds drawn from the Fed was 8.5 percentage points above the London Interbank Offered Rate (LIBOR), a rate that banks charge to lend to each other. AIG also was to pay a flat 8.5% interest rate on any funds that it did not draw from the facility. The government received warrants that, if exercised, would give the government a 79.9% ownership stake in AIG. Three independent trustees were to be named by the Fed to oversee the firm for the duration of the loan. The trustees for the AIG Credit Trust were announced on January 16, 2009, and the warrants were later exercised.[32]

This lending facility (and its successors) was secured by the assets of AIG's holding company and non-regulated subsidiaries.[33] In other words, the Fed could seize AIG's assets if AIG failed to honor the terms of the loan. This reduced the risk that the Fed, and the taxpayers, would suffer a loss, assuming, of course, that the Fed would have been willing to seize these assets. The risk still remained that if AIG turned out to be insolvent, its assets might be insufficient to cover the amount it had borrowed from the Fed.

On September 18, 2008, the Fed announced that it had initially lent $28 billion of the $85 billion possible. This amount grew to approximately $61 billion on November 5, 2008, shortly before the restructuring of the loan discussed below in "Federal Reserve Loan Restructuring."[34]

## Securities Borrowing Facility[35]

On October 8, 2008, the Fed announced that it was expanding its assistance to AIG by swapping cash for up to $37.8 billion of AIG's investment-grade, fixed-income securities. These securities stemmed from the AIG securities lending program. As some counterparties stopped participating in the lending program, AIG was forced to incur losses on its securities lending investments.[36] AIG needed liquidity from the Fed to cover these losses and counterparty withdrawals. This lending facility was to extend for nearly two years, until September 16, 2010, and advances from the securities borrowing facility to AIG paid an interest rate of 1% over the average overnight repo rate.[37] As of November 5, 2008, shortly before the facility was restructured, $19.9 billion of the $37.8 billion was outstanding.

Although this assistance resembled a typical collateralized loan (the lender receives assets as collateral, and the borrower receives cash), the Fed characterized the agreement as a loan of securities from AIG to the Fed in exchange for cash collateral. The arrangement may have been structured this way due to New York state insurance law provisions regarding insurers using securities as collateral in a loan.[38]

## Commercial Paper Funding Facility

The Commercial Paper Funding Facility (CPFF) was initially announced by the Fed on October 7, 2008, as a measure to restore liquidity in the commercial paper market.[39] It was a general facility, open to many recipients, not only AIG. Through the CPFF, the Fed purchased both asset-backed and unsecured commercial paper. Rather than charging an interest rate, the Fed purchased the paper at a discount based on the three-month overnight index swap rate (OIS). Unsecured paper was discounted by 3%, whereas secured paper was discounted by 1%.

AIG announced that, as of November 5, 2008, it had been authorized to issue up to $20.9 billion of commercial paper to the CPFF and had actually issued approximately $15.3 billion of this amount. Subsequent downgrades of AIG's airline leasing subsidiary (ILFC) reduced the maximum amount AIG could access from the CPFF to $15.2 billion in early January 2009. ILFC had approximately $1.7 billion outstanding to the CPFF when it was downgraded; this amount was repaid by January 28, 2009.[40]

On February 17, 2010, the reported total CPFF borrowing outstanding was $2.3 billion.[41] CPFF new purchase of commercial paper expired February 1, 2010, with maximum maturities extending 90 days from this point. Thus, by the end of April 2010, all AIG borrowing from the CPFF was repaid.

### Table A-1. Summary of AIG Assistance Before TARP

| Program | Maximum Committed Amount of Government Assistance | Government Assistance Outstanding (as Nov. 5, 2008) | Recompense to the Government | Expiration Date |
|---|---|---|---|---|
| Federal Reserve Loan Federal Reserve Securities Borrowing Facility Commercial Paper Funding Facility | $85 billion $37.8 billion $20.9 billion | $61 billion: (includes principal and interest) $19.9 billion: (includes principal and interest) $15.3 billion | LIBOR+8.5% (drawn amounts); 8.5% (undrawn amounts); 79.9% of AIG equity Overnight repo rate +1% OIS rate+1%; OIS+3% | September 2010 September 2010 February 2010 |

Source: Federal Reserve EESA Section 129 reports; AIG SEC filings.

## November 2008 Revision of Assistance to AIG

On November 10, 2008, the Federal Reserve and the U.S. Treasury announced a restructuring of the federal intervention to support AIG. Following the initial loan, some, notably AIG's former CEO Maurice Greenberg, criticized the terms as overly harsh, arguing that the loan itself might be contributing to AIG's eventual failure as a company. As evidenced by the additional borrowing after the September 16 loan, AIG had continued to see cash flow out of the company.

The revised agreement eased the payment terms for AIG and had three primary parts: (1) restructuring of the initial $85 billion Fed loan, (2) a $40 billion direct capital injection from the Treasury, and (3) up to $52.5 billion in Fed loans used to purchase troubled assets. Separately, AIG continued to access the Fed CPFF as described above.

### Federal Reserve Loan Restructuring

The Fed reduced the $85 billion loan facility to $60 billion, extended the time period to five years, and eased the financial terms considerably. Specifically, the interest rate on the amount outstanding was reduced by 5.5 percentage points (to LIBOR plus 3%), and the fee on the undrawn funds was reduced by 7.75 percentage points (to 0.75%).

### Troubled Asset Relief Program Assistance

Through TARP, the Treasury purchased $40 billion in preferred shares of AIG. In addition to the preferred shares, the Treasury also received warrants for common shares equal to 2% of the outstanding AIG shares. AIG was the first announced non-bank to receive TARP funds. The $40 billion in preferred AIG shares held by the Treasury were slated to pay a 10% dividend per annum, accrued quarterly.[42] The amount of shares held in trust for the benefit of the U.S. Treasury under the previous Fed loan was also reduced so that the total government equity interest in AIG (trust shares plus Treasury warrants) remained under 80% after the TARP intervention.

### Purchase of Troubled Assets

Although EESA provided for Treasury purchase of troubled assets under TARP, the troubled asset purchases related to AIG were done by LLCs created and controlled by the Federal Reserve. This structure was similar to that created by the Fed to facilitate the purchase of Bear Stearns by JPMorgan Chase in March 2008. Two LLCs were set up for AIG—Maiden Lane II for residential mortgage-backed securities (RMBS) and Maiden Lane III for collateralized debt obligations (CDO).[43]

### Residential Mortgage-Backed Securities/Maiden Lane II

Under the November 2008 restructuring, the RMBS LLC/Maiden Lane II could receive loans up to $22.5 billion by the Fed and $1 billion from AIG to purchase RMBS from AIG's securities lending portfolio. The previous $37.8 billion securities lending loan facility was repaid and terminated following the creation of this LLC. The Fed was credited with interest from its loan to Maiden Lane II at a rate of LIBOR plus 1% for a term of six years, extendable by the Fed. The $1 billion loan from AIG was credited with interest at a rate of LIBOR plus 3%. The AIG loan, however, was subordinate to the Fed's. Any proceeds from Maiden Lane II were to be distributed in the following order: (1) operating expenses of the LLC, (2) principal due to the Fed, (3) interest due to the Fed, and (4) deferred payment and interest due to AIG. Should additional funds remain at the liquidation of the LLC, these remaining funds were to be shared by the Fed and AIG with AIG receiving one-sixth of the value. Ultimately the securities in Maiden Lane II were sufficient to fully repay the loans, with interest. The Fed received approximately $2.3 billion in capital gains, with AIG receiving approximately $460 million

The actual amount of Fed loan made to Maiden Lane II totaled $19.5 billion of the $22.5 billion maximum. Maiden Lane II purchased RMBS with this amount along with the $1 billion loan from AIG. The securities purchased had a face value of nearly double the purchase price ($39.3 billion).[44]

### Collateralized Debt Obligations/Maiden Lane III

Under the November 2008 restructuring, the CDO LLC/Maiden Lane III could receive loans up to $30 billion from the Fed and $5 billion from AIG to purchase CDOs on which AIG had written credit default swaps. At the same time that the CDOs were purchased, the CDS written on these CDOs were terminated, relieving financial pressure on AIG. The Fed and AIG were to be credited with interest from the loans at a rate of LIBOR plus 3% until repaid. The proceeds from Maiden Lane III were to be distributed in the following order: (1) operating expenses of the LLC, (2) principal due to the Fed, (3) interest due to the Fed, and (4) deferred payment and interest due to AIG. Should any funds remain after this distribution, they were to go two-thirds to the Fed and one-third to AIG. Ultimately the securities in Maiden Lane III were sufficient to fully repay the loans, with interest. The Fed received approximately $5.9 billion in capital gains, with AIG receiving approximately $2.9 billion.

The actual amount of the Fed loan to Maiden Lane III was $24.3 billion of the $30 billion maximum, while AIG loaned the LLC $5 billion. In addition to these loans, Maiden Lane III purchase of CDOs was also funded by approximately $35 billion in cash collateral previously posted to holders of CDS by AIGFP. In return for the use of this collateral, AIGFP received approximately $2.5 billion from the LLC. The total par value of CDOs purchased by Maiden Lane III was approximately $62.1 billion.

**Table A-2. Summary of AIG Assistance Under November 2008 Plan (amounts as of March 2009)**

| Program | Maximum Committed Amount of Government Assistance | Government Assistance Outstanding | Recompense to the Government | Expiration Date |
|---|---|---|---|---|
| TARP Share Purchase | $40 billion | $40 billion (principal); $1.6 billion (dividends) | 10% quarterly dividend; warrants for 2% of AIG equity; | Preferred shares outstanding until repurchased. |
| Federal Reserve Loan | $60 billion | $42.0 billion (includes principal and interest) | 3 month LIBOR+3%; 77.9% of AIG equity | September 2013 |
| Commercial Paper Funding Facility | $20.9 billion | $12.2 billion $18.4 billion | OIS rate+1%; OIS+3% 5/6 of equity | October 2009 November 2014 |
| Maiden Lane II | $22.5 billion | (principal); $91 million (interest) $24.0 billion | remaining after loan repayment 2/3 of equity | (loan); assets held until disposed of. November 2014 |
| Maiden Lane III | $30 billion | (principal); $127 million (interest) | remaining after loan repayment | (loan); assets held until disposed of. |

Source: Federal Reserve weekly H.1.4 statistical release; Federal Reserve Bank of NY website; U.S. Treasury TARP reports; AIG SEC filings; CRS calculations.

Notes: CPFF and TARP values as of March 31, 2009, other Fed values as of March 25, 2009. The loan amounts to Maiden Lane II and III were from these entities to the Fed, and were not to be repaid by AIG. AIG also had outstanding loans Maiden Lane II and III, which were junior in priority to the Fed loans. The dividends on the TARP share purchase and the interest on the loans were generally allowed to accrue rather than being immediately paid.

A summary of the assistance under the November 2008 plan is presented in *Table A-2*.

## March 2009 Revision of Assistance to AIG

On March 2, 2009, the Treasury and Fed announced another revision of the financial assistance to AIG. On the same day, AIG announced a loss of more than $60 billion in the fourth quarter of 2008. In response to the poor results and ongoing financial turmoil, private credit ratings agencies were reportedly considering further downgrading AIG, which would most likely have resulted in further significant cash demands due to collateral calls.[45] According to the Treasury, AIG "continues to face significant challenges, driven by the rapid deterioration in certain financial markets in the last two months of the year and continued turbulence in the markets generally." The revised assistance was intended to "enhance the company's capital and liquidity in order to facilitate the orderly completion of the company's global divestiture program."[46]

The announced revised assistance included the following:

- Exchange of the previous $40 billion in preferred shares purchased through the TARP program for $41.6 billion in preferred shares that more closely resembled common equity, thus improving AIG's financial position. Dividends paid on these new shares remained at 10%, but were non-cumulative and only paid when declared by AIG's Board of Directors. Should dividends not be paid for four consecutive quarters, the government would have had the right to appoint at least two new directors to the board.
- Commitment of up to $29.8 billion[47] in additional preferred share purchases from TARP. Timing of these share purchases was at the discretion of AIG.
- Reduction of interest rate on the existing Fed loan facility by removing the floor of 3.5% over the LIBOR portion of the rate. The rate became three-month LIBOR plus 3%, which was approximately 4.25% at the time.
- Limit on Fed revolving credit facility was reduced from $60 billion to as low as $25 billion.
- Up to $34.5 billion of the approximately $38 billion outstanding on the Fed credit facility was to be repaid by asset transfers from AIG to the

Fed. Specifically, (1) $8.5 billion in ongoing life insurance cash flows were to be securitized by AIG and transferred to the Fed; and (2) approximately $26 billion in equity interests in two of AIG's large foreign life insurance subsidiaries (ALICO and AIA) are to be issued to the Fed. This would effectively transfer a majority stake in these companies to the Fed, but the companies would still be managed by AIG.

A $25 billion repayment of the Fed loan through the transfer of equity interest worth $16 billion in AIA and $9 billion in ALICO was completed on December 1, 2009, with a corresponding reduction in the Fed loan maximum to $35 billion. According to AIG's 2009 annual 10-K filing with the SEC, the repayment through securitization of life insurance cash flows was no longer expected to occur and has not occurred.

Separately, AIG continued to access the Fed's Commercial Paper Funding Facility, which was extended to February 2010.

A summary of assistance under the March 2009 plan is presented in *Table A-3*.

### Table A-3. Summary of AIG Assistance Under March 2009 Plan (amounts as of September 2010)

| Program | Maximum Committed Amount of Government Assistance | Government Assistance Outstanding | Recompense to the Government | Expiration Date |
|---------|------------------------------------------------|----------------------------------|------------------------------|-----------------|
| TARP Share Purchase | $69.8 billion | $47.5 billion (principal); $1.6 billion (dividends) | 10% quarterly dividend; warrants for 2% of AIG equity | March 2014; preferred shares outstanding until repurchased |
| Federal Reserve Loan | $35 billion | $18.9 billion: (includes principal and interest) | 3 month LIBOR+3%; 77.9% of AIG equity | September 2013 |
| AIG Subsidiary Equity (accepted as repayment for Fed Loan) | $25 billion | $25 billion (principal); $1 billion (dividends) | 5% quarterly dividends | none |

**Table A-3. (Continued)**

| Program | Maximum Committed Amount of Government Assistance | Government Assistance Outstanding | Recompense to the Government | Expiration Date |
|---|---|---|---|---|
| Commercial Paper Funding Facility | $15.9 billion | $0 (facility expired) | OIS rate+1%; OIS+3% | February 2010 |
| Maiden Lane II | $22.5 billion | $13.7 billion (principal); $408 million (interest) | 5/6 of equity remaining after loan repayment | November 2014 (loan); assets held until disposed of |
| Maiden Lane III | $30 billion | $14.6 billion (principal); $499 million (interest) | 2/3 of equity remaining after loan repayment | November 2014 (loan); assets held until disposed of |

Source: Federal Reserve weekly H.1.4 statistical release; Federal Reserve Bank of NY
   website; U.S. Treasury TARP reports; AIG SEC filings; CRS calculations.
Notes: Fed amounts as of September 29, 2010; Treasury amounts as of September 30,
   2010. The loan amounts to Maiden Lane II and III were from these entities to the
   Fed, and were not to be repaid by AIG. AIG also has outstanding loans Maiden
   Lane II and III which were junior in priority to the Fed loans. Quarterly TARP
   dividends were non-cumulative and paid at AIG's discretion. The dividends on the
   TARP share purchase and the interest on the loans were generally allowed to
   accrue rather than being immediately paid.

## September 2010 Revision of Assistance for AIG

The structure under which AIG's assistance was ultimately wound down
was announced in September 2010 with the multiple transactions involved
closing on January 14, 2011. The essence of this restructuring was to (1) end
the Fed's direct involvement with AIG through loan repayment and transfer of
the Fed's equity interests to the Treasury and (2) convert the government's
preferred shares into common shares, which could then be more easily sold.
The specific steps included the following:

- Repayment and termination of the Fed loan facility. AIG repaid $19.5
  billion to the Fed with cash from the disposal of various assets.

- Transfer to the Treasury of the Fed's preferred equity interests resulting from AIG subsidiaries AIA and Alico. AIG drew $20.3 billion of TARP funds to purchase the Fed's equity in AIG's subsidiaries. This equity was transferred to the Treasury to redeem the TARP funds. The remaining equity (approximately $5.7 billion) was redeemed by funds from sales of other AIG assets. As was the plan when the Fed held the assets, the equity interests held by the Treasury following the transfer were to be redeemed by AIG following further asset sales.

- *Conversion of TARP preferred shares into common equity.* $49.1 billion in TARP preferred share holdings were converted into approximately 1.1 billion common shares worth approximately $43 billion in September 2010.[48] After combining this with the approximately 562.9 million shares (then worth $22 billion) resulting from the initial Fed loan,[49] the Treasury held 1.655 billion shares of AIG common stock, or 92.1% of the AIG common stock.

- *Reduced TARP funding facility.* At AIG's discretion, $2 billion of new Series G preferred shares could be issued by AIG and purchased by the Treasury. These shares would have paid a 5% dividend and any outstanding shares were to convert to common shares at the end of March 2012. None of these shares were issued and this facility was cancelled.

- *Issuance of warrants to private shareholders.* Through an exceptional dividend, AIG issued warrants to existing private shareholders. They extend for 10 years and allow for the purchase of up to 75 million new shares of common stock at the price of $45 a share. These warrants provided a direct benefit to private AIG stockholders while potentially reducing the return on the government's assistance to AIG. This benefit was approximately $1.2 billion at the warrant's initial trading price.[50]

*Table 5* summarizes the assistance for AIG after the latest restructuring plan was completed in January 2011, but before any further asset sales or loan repayments.

**Table A-4. Summary of AIG Assistance Under Final September 2010 Plan (after closing in mid-January 2011)**

| Agency | Holdings | Amount | Planned Disposition | Original Source |
|---|---|---|---|---|
| Treasury | AIG common equity | 1.655 billion shares (worth approximately $71.5 billion) | Open market sales | $49.1 billion in TARP preferred shares were converted to 1.1 billion shares; 563 million shares were compensation for Fed loan to AIG (transferred through AIG Credit Trust) |
| | AIG subsidiary equity | $20.3 billion | Redemption by AIG through equity sales | Fed loan to AIG (transferred using TARP preferred shares) |
| | AIG preferred shares | $0 (of up to $2 billion) | Redemption by AIG or conversion to common equity | Purchased through TARP |
| Federal Reserve | Maiden Lane II Maiden Lane III | $12.8 billion (principal); $460 million (interest); $1.4 billion (equity) $12.7 billion (principal); $555 million (interest); $2.6 billion (equity) | Hold to maturity or open market sale Hold to maturity or open market sale | Fed loan to Maiden Lane II Fed loan to Maiden Lane III |

Source: Federal Reserve weekly H.4.1 statistical release; Federal Reserve Bank of NY website; U.S. Treasury TARP reports and press releases; AIG SEC filings; CRS calculations.

Note: Values from January 20, 2011.

# APPENDIX B. EXECUTIVE COMPENSATION RESTRICTIONS UNDER TARP

By accepting TARP assistance, AIG became subject to the executive compensation standards for their senior executive officers (SEOs, generally the chief executive officer, the chief financial, and the three next most highly compensated officials) generally required under Section 111 of EESA. In addition to these general restrictions, Treasury imposed additional executive compensation restrictions on AIG that are more stringent than for other participants in TARP in recognition of the special assistance received by AIG.[51]

The TARP executive compensation restrictions were amended and strengthened by the 111th Congress in the American Recovery and Reinvestment Act of 2009,[52] which amended Section 111 of EESA to further limit executive compensation for financial institutions receiving assistance under that act. Among other things, for applicable companies, the new language requires the adoption of standards by Treasury that

1. prohibit paying certain executives any bonus, retention, or incentive compensation other than certain long-term restricted stock that has a value not greater than one-third of the total annual compensation of the employee receiving the stock (the determination of how many executives will be subject to these limitations depends on the amount of funds received by the TARP recipient);

2. require the recovery of any bonus, retention award, or incentive compensation paid to SEOs and the next 20 most highly compensated employees based on earnings, revenues, gains, or other criteria that are later found to be materially inaccurate;

3. prohibit any compensation plan that would encourage manipulation of the reported earnings of the firm to enhance the compensation of any of its employees;

4. prohibit the provision of "golden parachute" payment to an SEO and the next five most highly compensated employees for departure from a company for any reason, except for payments for services performed or benefits accrued; and

5. prohibit any compensation plan that would encourage manipulation of the reported earnings of the firm to enhance the compensation of any of its employees.

Although Section 111(b)(1) of the amended EESA indicated that these standards applied all TARP recipients until they repay TARP funding, later language (Section 111(b)(3)(iii)) specifically allows bonuses required to be paid under employment contracts executed before February 11, 2009, to go forward notwithstanding the new requirements. The Special Master for TARP Executive Compensation released several specific determinations for AIG compensation.[53]

## End Notes

[1] Statistics from The I.I.I. Insurance Fact Book 2009, (New York: Insurance Information Institute, 2009).

[2] P.L. 79-15, 15 U.S.C. §§1011-1015.

[3] In 2005, amid accounting irregularities that ultimately led to the resignation of then-CEO Maurice Greenberg, AIG was downgraded by S&P from AAA to AA+. Further downgrades followed in June 2005 and May 2008. In September 2008, S&P downgraded AIG to A-.

[4] See, for example, "U.S. to Take Over AIG in $85 Billion Bailout; Central Banks Inject Cash as Credit Dries Up," Wall Street Journal, September 17, 2008, pp. A1-A6.

[5] Institutions that are too big to fail are ones that are deemed to be big enough, or interconnected enough, that their failure could create systemic risk, the risk that the financial system as a whole would cease to function smoothly. See CRS Report R40877, Financial Regulatory Reform: Systemic Risk and the Federal Reserve, by Marc Labonte and CRS Report R40417, Macroprudential Oversight: Monitoring Systemic Risk in the Financial System, by Darryl E. Getter for more information on systemic risk and "too big to fail."

[6] The revisions point to a fundamental trade-off between making the terms of the assistance undesirable enough to deter other firms from seeking government assistance and making the terms of assistance so punitive that they exacerbate the financial problems of the recipient firm. It also points to the risk that once a firm has been identified as too big to fail, government assistance to the firm can become open-ended.

[7] P.L. 111-203.

[8] The AIGFP derivatives operation was wound down and largely discontinued. If AIG were to again undertake such an operation, it would fall under the oversight of the Fed.

[9] See http://www.treasury.gov/initiatives/fsoc/designations/ Documents/Basis% 20of%20Final %20Determination%20Regarding%20American%20International%20Group,%20Inc.pdf.

[10] See the committee website at http://oversight.house.gov/hearings/?committees=subcommittee-on-economic-growthjob-creation-and-regulatory-affairs.

[11] For additional detail, please see the section entitled "Who Has Benefited from Assistance to AIG?," in CRS Report R40438, Federal Government Assistance for American International Group (AIG), by Baird Webel, pp. 14-15.

[12] For more information on the Starr lawsuits see CRS Sidebar WSLG271, AIG's Former CEO's $20 Billion Illegal Exaction Claim Based on Federal Reserve's "Illegal" Financial Assistance, by M. Maureen Murphy and CRS Report WSLG366, AIG's Board Will Not Join Shareholder Suits Against Treasury and Federal Reserve, by M. Maureen Murphy.

[13] American International Group, "AIG Repurchases Warrants from U.S. Treasury," press release, March 1, 2013, http://www.aig.com/press-releases_3171_438003.html.

[14] The rate varied between 12% and 12.55% before it was reduced after November 2008.

[15] See CRS Report RL30354, *Monetary Policy and the Federal Reserve: Current Policy and Conditions*, by Marc Labonte for more information on the Federal Reserve.

[16] A similar LLC, known simply as Maiden Lane, was created to address the failure of the investment bank Bear Stearns in March 2008. The name "Maiden Lane" derives from one of the streets bordering the Federal Reserve Bank of New York headquarters in Manhattan.

[17] AIG also contributed a total of $6 billion to the LLCs and they were structured so that AIG's contribution would bear initial losses, should losses occur. Because of this contribution, AIG shared in the gains that eventually occurred as well. AIG's share was one-sixth of the gains in Maiden Lane II and one-third in Maiden Lane III.

[18] See CRS Report RL34427, *Financial Turmoil: Federal Reserve Policy Responses*, by Marc Labonte for more information on CPFF.

[19] The CPFF interest rates ranged from 2% to 3% compared with as high as 12.5% on the regular Fed loan facility.

[20] This reporting can be found on the Federal Reserve webpage at http://www.federalreserve.gov/newsevents/ reform_cpff.htm and the figures presented here are based on this data.

[21] Preferred equity is a "hybrid" form of equity that confers no management rights with respect to the company and pays some form of dividend. It performs similarly to a loan in economic terms, but is accounted for as equity, thus improves the capital position of an institution more than a loan. As equity, preferred shares would be junior to debt, thus holdings in preferred equity would be riskier than the equivalent amount of a loan.

[22] The second large tranche of TARP assistance was used to transfer to the Treasury the AIG subsidiary equity, which the Fed had previously accepted as partial loan repayment and to partially repay the outstanding cash balance on the Fed loan.

[23] Warrants were issued in 2008 and 2009. According to AIG, "The warrant issued in 2008 provided the right to purchase approximately 2.7 million shares of AIG common stock at $50.00 per share, and the warrant issued in 2009 provided the right to purchase up to 150 shares of AIG common stock at $0.00002 per share." See http://www.aig.com/ press-releases_3171_438003.html.

[24] The IRS issued several notices on this issue, including Notice 2008-100, I.R.B. 2008-44, October 14, 2008; Notice 2009-14, I.R.B. 2009-7, January 30, 2009; Notice 2009-38, I.R.B. 2009-18, April 13, 2009; and Notice 2010-2, I.R.B. 2010-2, December 14, 2009.

[25] The tax code generally does not permit such assumption of tax losses in order to discourage companies from making acquisitions solely for the purpose of assuming tax losses.

[26] American International Group, Inc., 2011 Annual Report (SEC Form 10-K, February 23, 2012, p. 62.

[27] See, for example, http://www.treasury.gov/connect/blog/Pages/AIG-wrapup.aspx.

[28] 2 U.S.C. 661 et.seq; more information available in CRS Report RL30346, *Federal Credit Reform: Implementation of the Changed Budgetary Treatment of Direct Loans and Loan Guarantees*, by James M. Bickley (out of print, but available from the author). This law requires the present value of the full long-term cost of loans and loan guarantees be recognized in the federal budget when the loans or loan guarantees are made.

[29] These requirements were contained in the Emergency Economic Stabilization Act (P.L. 110-343, codified at 12 U.S.C. 5233) and apply to all TARP assistance.

[30] CBO, Report on the Troubled Asset Relief Program—May 2013, May 23, 2013, p. 6, available at http://cbo.gov/sites/ default/files/cbofiles/attachments/44256_TARP.pdf.

[31] CBO, The Budgetary Impact And Subsidy Costs Of The Federal Reserve's Actions During The Financial Crisis, May 24, 2010, p. 8, available at http://www.cbo.gov/sites/default/ files/cbofiles/ftpdocs/115xx/doc11524/05-24- federalreserve.pdf.

[32] See http://www.newyorkfed.org/newsevents/news/markets/2009/an090116.html.

[33] The regulated subsidiaries were primarily the state-chartered insurance subsidiaries. Thus, if AIG had defaulted on the loan, the Fed could have seized the insurance subsidiary stock held by the holding company, but not the actual assets held by the insurance companies.

[34] Federal Reserve, "Factors Affecting Reserve Balances," Statistical Release H.4.1, September 18, 2008. See http://www.federalreserve.gov/releases/h41/20080918/; and "Report Pursuant to Section 129 of the Emergency Economic Stabilization Act of 2008: Restructuring of the Government's Financial Support to the American International Group, Inc. on November 10, 2008, p. 4. See http://www.federalreserve.gov/monetarypolicy/files/ 129aigres tructure.pdf.

[35] Terms detailed by the Federal Reserve in "Report Pursuant to Section 129 of the Emergency Economic Stabilization Act of 2008: Securities Borrowing Facility for American International Group, Inc.," available at http://www.federalreserve.gov/monetarypolicy/ files/129aigsecborrowfacility.pdf.

[36] Liam Pleven et al, "AIG Bailout Hit by New Cash Woes," Wall Street Journal, October 9, 2008, p. A1.

[37] A "repo" is an agreement for the sale and repurchase of a particular security, with an overnight repo being a short term example of such a contract.

[38] N.Y. Ins. Law, Section 1410.

[39] Commercial paper is an unsecured promissory note with relatively short term maturity, typically 1 to 15 days, sold by corporations to meet immediate funding needs.

[40] American International Group, Inc., 2008 Annual Report (SEC Form 10-K), March 2, 2009.

[41] American International Group, Inc., "AIG Reports Fourth Quarter and Full Year 2009 Results," press release, February 26, 2010, p. 5, available at http://phx.corporate-ir.net/External.File?item= UGFyZW50SUQ9MzM3MjR8Q2hpbGRJ RD0tMXxUe XBlP TM=&t=1.

[42] Full details of the preferred shares can be found on the Treasury website at http://ustreas.gov/press/releases/reports/ 111008aigtermsheet.pdf.

[43] The headquarters of the Federal Reserve Bank of New York sits between Maiden Lane and Liberty Street in downtown New York City.

[44] "Maiden Lane Transactions" on the webpage of the Federal Reserve Bank of New York, available at http://www.newyorkfed.org/markets/maidenlane.html#maidenlane2.

[45] See, for example, "A.I.G. Reports Loss of $61.7 Billion as U.S. Gives More Aid," New York Times, March 2, 2009, p. A1.

[46] U.S. Treasury, "U.S. Treasury and Federal Reserve Board Announce Participation in AIG Restructuring Plan," press release, March 2, 2009.

[47] The amount was reduced from $30 billion following controversy over $165 million in employee bonuses paid to AIGFP employees in March 2009.

[48] According to The Wall Street Journal, AIG's common stock closed at a price of $39.10 on September 30, 2010.

[49] This equity was previously held by the AIG Credit Trust and was transferred to the Treasury with the dissolution of the trust.

[50] The warrants were trading for approximately $16.05 on January 20, 2011. See http://dealbook.nytimes.com/2011/01/ 20/about-a-i-g-s-stock-price/.

[51] U.S. Treasury, "Treasury to Invest in AIG Restructuring under the Emergency Economic Stabilization Act," hp-1261, November 10, 2008, available at http://www.ustreas.gov/press/releases/hp1261.htm.

[52] Section 7001 of P.L. 111-5.

[53] See "Executive Compensation" on the Treasury Financialstability.gov website available at http://www.financialstability.gov/about/executivecompensation.html.

In: Money, Economics, and Finance. Volume 3     ISBN: 978-1-63321-505-4
Editor: Clifford Dobrowski                © 2014 Nova Science Publishers, Inc.

*Chapter 6*

# INVESTMENT ADVISERS: REQUIREMENTS AND COSTS ASSOCIATED WITH THE CUSTODY RULE*

## *United States Government Accountability Office*

## WHY GAO DID THIS STUDY

Investment advisers provide a wide range of services and collectively manage around $54 trillion in assets for around 24 million clients. Unlike banks and broker-dealers, investment advisers typically do not maintain physical custody of client assets. However, under federal securities regulations, advisers may be deemed to have custody because of their authority to access client assets, for example, by deducting advisory fees from a client account. High-profile fraud cases in recent years highlighted the risks faced by investors when an adviser has custody of their assets. In response, SEC amended its custody rule in 2009 to require a broader range of advisers to undergo annual surprise examinations by independent accountants. At the same time, SEC provided relief from this requirement to certain advisers, including those deemed to have custody solely because of their use of related but "operationally independent" custodians. The Dodd-Frank Wall Street Reform and Consumer Protection Act mandates GAO to study the costs

---

\* This is an edited, reformatted and augmented version of a United States Government Accountability Office publication, No. GAO-13-569, dated July 2013.

associated with the custody rule. This report describes (1) the requirements of and costs associated with the custody rule and (2) SEC's rationale for not requiring advisers using related but operationally independent custodians to undergo surprise examinations.

To address the objectives, GAO reviewed federal securities laws and related rules, analyzed data on advisers, and met with SEC, advisers, accounting firms, and industry and other associations.

# WHAT GAO FOUND

Designed to safeguard client assets, the Securities and Exchange Commission's (SEC) rule governing advisers' custody of client assets (custody rule) imposes various requirements and, in turn, costs on investment advisers. To protect investors, the rule requires advisers that have custody to (1) use qualified custodians (e.g., banks or broker-dealers) to hold client assets and (2) have a reasonable basis for believing that the custodian sends account statements directly to clients.

The rule also requires advisers with custody, unless they qualify for an exception, to hire an independent public accountant to conduct annually a surprise examination to verify custody of client assets. According to accountants that GAO interviewed, examination cost depends on an adviser's number of clients under custody and other factors. These factors vary widely across advisers that currently report undergoing surprise examinations: for example, their reported number of clients under custody ranged from 1 client to over 1 million clients as of April 2013. Thus, the cost of the examinations varies widely across the advisers. The rule also requires advisers maintaining client assets or using a qualified custodian that is a related person to obtain an internal control report to assess the suitability and effectiveness of controls in place. The cost of these reports varies across custodians based on their size and services.

SEC provided an exception from the surprise examination requirement to, among others, advisers deemed to have custody solely because of their use of related but "operationally independent" custodians. According to SEC, an adviser and custodian under common ownership but having operationally independent management pose relatively lower client custodial risks, because the misuse of client assets would tend to require collusion between the firms' employees. To be considered operationally independent, an adviser and its related custodian must not be under common supervision, not share premises, and meet other conditions. About 2 percent of the SEC-registered advisers qualify for this exception for at least some of their clients. If the exception were eliminated, the cost of the surprise examination would vary across the advisers because the factors that affect examination cost vary widely across the advisers.

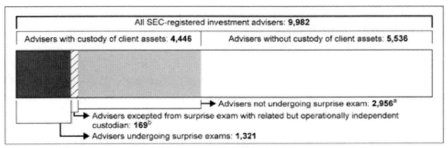

Source: GAO analysis of Form ADV data as of April 1, 2013.

[a] These advisers may undergo an annual financial statement audit in lieu of a surprise examination.

[b] Of the 169 SEC-registered investment advisers excepted from the surprise examination requirement, 41 of them qualified for an exception from the surprise examination requirement for some of their clients under custody but underwent a surprise examination for other clients under custody.

Number of SEC-Registered Investment Advisers, as of April 2013.

## ABBREVIATIONS

| | |
|---|---|
| IARD | Investment Adviser Registration Depository |
| NASAA | North American Securities Administrators Association |
| PCAOB | Public Company Accounting Oversight Board |
| SEC | Securities and Exchange Commission |

July 8, 2013

The Honorable Tim Johnson
Chairman
The Honorable Mike Crapo
Ranking Member
Committee on Banking,

Housing, and Urban Affairs
United States Senate

The Honorable Jeb Hensarling
Chairman
The Honorable Maxine Waters
Ranking Member
Committee on Financial Services
House of Representatives

Investment advisers provide a wide range of investment advisory services and collectively manage around $54 trillion in assets for about 24 million clients. Unlike banks and broker-dealers, investment advisers typically do not maintain physical custody of client assets—that is, client funds and securities. However, under federal securities regulations, advisers may be deemed to have custody because of their authority to access client assets, for example, by deducting advisory fees from a client account.[1] The collapse of Bernard L. Madoff Investment Securities, LLC—an investment adviser and broker-dealer—in December 2008 resulted in thousands of investors losing over $50 billion and highlighted the risks investors face when an adviser has custody of client funds and securities.

Under the Securities and Exchange Commission's (SEC) custody rule, advisers that have custody of client assets are required to implement controls designed to protect those assets from being lost, misused, misappropriated, or subject to the advisers' financial reverses, such as insolvency.[2] SEC first adopted the custody rule in 1962, after Congress amended the Investment Advisers Act of 1940 (Advisers Act) in 1960 to give it authority to promulgate rules to define and prescribe means reasonably designed to prevent fraudulent, deceptive, or manipulative acts, practices, or courses of business.[3] At that time, the rule generally required, among other things, that advisers with custody hire an independent public accountant to conduct an annual surprise examination to verify custody of client assets. In 2003, SEC amended the rule to require advisers to adopt new controls to protect client assets and relieve certain advisers from the surprise examination requirement.[4] In response to the Madoff and other recent frauds, SEC amended the rule again in 2009 to improve the safekeeping of client assets—in part by expanding the surprise examination requirement's reach.[5] As noted by SEC in its 2009 final rule adopting release, surprise examinations provide "another set of eyes" on client assets and thus additional protection against their misappropriation. Under the amended rule, SEC continued to provide an exception from the surprise examination requirement to certain advisers, including advisers that have custody solely because of their use of related but "operationally independent" custodians to hold client assets.[6]

Section 412 of the Dodd-Frank Wall Street Reform and Consumer Protection Act mandates us to study the costs that investment advisers registered with SEC incur to comply with SEC's record-keeping and custody rules, as well as the additional costs that advisers would incur if the operationally independent exception were eliminated.[7] This report describes

- the requirements of and costs associated with the SEC custody rule, including any related record-keeping requirements, for registered investment advisers; and
- SEC's rationale for not requiring advisers using related but operationally independent custodians to undergo surprise examinations, and the number and characteristics of such advisers.

To address these objectives, we reviewed and analyzed the Advisers Act and related regulations; proposed and final amendments made to SEC's custody rule, including comment letters; and relevant GAO, SEC, industry, and academic studies on investment advisers. We also analyzed publicly available Form ADV data filed by investment advisers to determine, among other things, the number of SEC-registered investment advisers that reported complying with certain custody rule requirements, including the surprise examination requirement, and assess the characteristics of certain investment advisers.[8] We interviewed SEC staff about the controls and procedures used to ensure the reliability of the data and found the data to be sufficiently reliable for the purposes of our report.

To obtain data on costs of complying with the SEC custody rule, particularly its surprise examination and internal control report requirements, we selected 12 investment advisers based on the number of their client accounts and amount of assets under custody. We interviewed eight of the advisers and four accounting firms that had conducted surprise examinations for the 12 selected advisers to obtain data on surprise examination costs and, if applicable, internal control reports. To obtain information about the requirements, costs, and other issues associated with the SEC custody rule, we interviewed, among others, federal and state regulators and representatives from various industry and other associations. (See app. I for more information about our scope and methodology.)

We conducted this performance audit from September 2012 through July 2013 in accordance with generally accepted government auditing standards. Those standards require that we plan and perform the audit to obtain sufficient, appropriate evidence to provide a reasonable basis for our findings and conclusions based on our audit objectives. We believe that the evidence obtained provides a reasonable basis for our findings and conclusions based on our audit objectives.

## BACKGROUND

Investment advisers provide a wide range of investment advisory services and help individuals and institutions make financial decisions.[9] From individuals and families seeking to plan for retirement or save for college to large institutions managing billions of dollars, clients seek the services of investment advisers to help them evaluate their investment needs, plan for their future, and develop and implement investment strategies. Advisers can include money managers, investment consultants, and financial planners. They commonly manage the investment portfolios of individuals, businesses, and pooled investment vehicles, such as mutual funds, pension funds, and hedge and other private funds. Many investment advisers also engage in other businesses, such as insurance broker or broker-dealer services. Many investment advisers charge clients fees for investment advisory services based on the percentage of assets under management, but others may charge hourly or fixed rates and, in certain circumstances, performance fees.

The Advisers Act generally defines an investment adviser, with certain exceptions, as any individual or firm that for compensation engages in the business of advising others, either directly or through publications or writings, as to the value of securities or as to the advisability of investing in, purchasing, or selling securities. 10 An entity that falls within the definition of "investment adviser" must register under the Advisers Act, unless it (1) is a small firm regulated by one or more of the states and thus prohibited from registering or (2) qualifies for an exemption from the Advisers Act's registration requirement.[11] The Advisers Act imposes a broad fiduciary duty on advisers to act in the best interest of their clients.

Most small- and mid-sized advisers are regulated by the states and prohibited from registering with SEC. 12 Large advisers who do not meet an exemption from registration must register with SEC. To register, applicants file a Form ADV with SEC. Once registered, an adviser must update the form at least annually. SEC-registered advisers are subject to five types of requirements: (1) fiduciary duties to clients; (2) substantive prohibitions and requirements, including that advisers with custody of client assets take steps designed to safeguard those client assets; (3) contractual requirements; (4) record-keeping requirements; and (5) oversight by SEC.

SEC oversees registered investment advisers primarily through its Office of Compliance Inspections and Examinations, Division of Investment Management, and Division of Enforcement. Specifically, the Office of Compliance Inspections and Examinations examines investment advisers to evaluate their compliance with federal securities laws, determines whether these firms are fulfilling their fiduciary duty to clients and operating in accordance with disclosures made to investors and contractual obligations, and assesses the effectiveness of their compliance-control systems. The Division of Investment Management administers the securities laws affecting investment advisers and engages in rule making for consideration by SEC and other policy initiatives that are intended, among other things, to strengthen SEC's oversight of investment advisers. The Division of Enforcement investigates and prosecutes certain violations of securities laws and regulations.

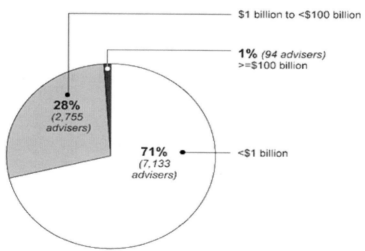

Source: GAO analysis of Form ADV data as of April 1, 2013.

Notes: Regulatory assets under management are the sum of assets under management or securities portfolios for which the adviser provides continuous and regular supervisory or management services and include, for accounts of private funds, the amount of any uncalled capital commitments as of the date of filing.

Advisers are instructed to determine the amount based on the current market value of the assets as determined within 90 days prior to the date of filing.

Figure 1. Percentage of SEC-Registered Advisers by Amount of Regulatory Assets under Management, as of April 1, 2013.

Nearly 10,000 advisers were registered with SEC as of April 1, 2013.[13] Collectively, these advisers managed nearly $54 trillion in assets for about 24 million clients. The majority of these SEC-registered advisers each managed less than $1 billion in assets, and a majority had 100 or fewer clients. Specifically, as shown in figure 1, about 71 percent of the registered advisers (around 7,133 advisers) managed less than $1 billion in assets. Furthermore, the largest 94 registered advisers (about 1 percent of all SEC-registered advisers) managed about 50 percent of the total regulatory assets under management.

In addition, as shown in figure 2, about 6,000 registered advisers (nearly 60 percent of all registered advisers) reported having 100 or fewer clients, while approximately 1,200 advisers (around 12 percent of all registered advisers) reported having more than 500 clients.

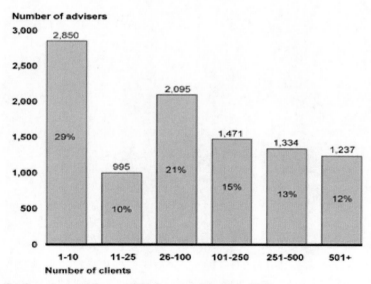

Source: GAO analysis of Form ADV data as of April 1, 2013.

Figure 2. Distribution of SEC-Registered Advisers by Number of Clients, as of April 1, 2013.

# CUSTODY RULE REQUIREMENTS AND COMPLIANCE COSTS VARY ACROSS ADVISERS

SEC-registered investment advisers with custody of client assets are required by the SEC custody rule to comply with a number of requirements designed to safeguard client assets. Under the rule, an adviser has custody if it holds, directly or indirectly, client funds or securities or has any authority to obtain possession of them.[14] An adviser also has custody if a related person of the adviser holds, directly or indirectly, client funds or securities or has any authority to obtain possession of them, in connection with advisory services provided by the adviser to the client.[15] Custody includes:

- possession of client funds or securities;
- any capacity that gives the adviser legal ownership or access to client assets, for example, as a general partner of a limited partnership, managing member of a limited liability company, or a comparable position for another pooled investment vehicle (e.g., hedge fund); or
- any arrangement, including a general power of attorney, under which the adviser is authorized or permitted to withdraw client funds or securities maintained with a custodian upon its instruction to the custodian.

## Custody Rule Requirements Are Intended to Safeguard Client Assets

SEC's custody rule regulates the custody practices of investment advisers and contains a number of investor protections. The rule requires advisers that have custody to maintain client assets with a "qualified custodian," which includes banks and savings associations, registered broker-dealers, registered futures commission merchants, and certain foreign financial institutions.[16] This requirement, along with other parts of the rule, helps prevent client assets from being lost or stolen. Furthermore, qualified custodians are subject to regulation and oversight by federal financial regulators and self-regulatory organizations.[17] Some registered advisers also engage in other businesses, such as broker-dealers that provide custodial services to themselves or related advisers.

The rule requires advisers that have custody of client assets to have a reasonable basis, after due inquiry, for believing that the custodian sends periodic statements directly to the clients.[18] An adviser can satisfy the due-inquiry requirement in a number of ways, such as by receiving a copy of the account statements sent to the clients or written confirmation from the custodian that account statements were sent to the adviser's clients. This requirement serves to help assure the integrity of account statements and permit clients to identify any erroneous or unauthorized transactions or withdrawals by an adviser. If an adviser also elects to send its own clients account statements, it must include a note urging its clients to compare the custodian's and adviser's account statements.

### *Surprise Examinations*

The SEC custody rule requires advisers with custody of client assets to hire an independent public accountant to conduct an annual surprise examination, unless the advisers qualify for an exception. [19] A surprise examination is intended to help deter and detect fraudulent activity by having an independent accountant verify that client assets—of which an adviser has custody—are held by a qualified custodian in an appropriate account and in the correct amount. The accountant determines the time of the examination without prior notice to the adviser, and the accountant is to vary the timing of the examination from year to year. SEC initially required all advisers to undergo surprise examinations when it adopted the custody rule in 1962.[20] Over the following decades of administering the custody rule, SEC staff provided no-action relief from the surprise examination requirement where other substitute client safeguards were implemented. In 2003, SEC amended the custody rule by generally requiring an adviser to maintain client assets with qualified custodians and relieving the adviser from the examination requirement if its qualified custodian sent account statements directly to the adviser's clients.[21] In its proposed rule at that time, SEC noted that the examination was performed only annually, and many months could pass before the accountant had an opportunity to detect a fraud.[22] In its 2009 proposed amendments, SEC revisited the 2003 rule making in light of its significant enforcement actions alleging misappropriation of client assets.[23] In expanding the surprise examination requirement, SEC noted that an independent public accountant may identify misuse that clients have not, which would result in the earlier detection of fraudulent activities and reduce resulting client losses.[24]

While SEC expanded the reach of the surprise examination requirement in its final 2009 rule amendments, it provided several exceptions to the requirement. As shown in figure 3, advisers meeting the following conditions may not be required to undergo a surprise examination:

- an adviser that is deemed to have custody of client assets solely because of its authority to deduct fees from client accounts;
- an adviser that is deemed to have custody because a related person has custody, and the adviser is "operationally independent" of the related person serving as the custodian;[25] or
- an adviser to a pooled investment vehicle (e.g., hedge fund) that is subject to an annual financial statement audit by an independent public accountant registered with and subject to regular inspection by the Public Company Accounting Oversight Board (PCAOB) and distributes the audited financial statements prepared in accordance with generally accepted accounting principles to its clients is deemed to have satisfied the surprise examination requirement.[26]

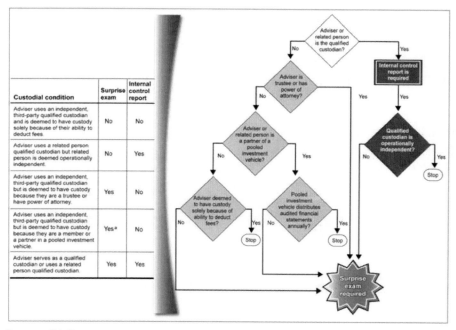

Source: GAO.

<sup>a</sup>Advisers to pooled investment vehicles may be deemed to comply with the surprise examination requirement of the vehicle if it is audited annually, the audited financial statements are distributed to investors annually, and the auditing is conducted by an independent public accountant that is PCAOB-registered and subject to regular inspection.

Figure 3. Exceptions to the Surprise Examination or Internal Control Report Requirements.

### *Internal Control Reports*

Advisers that maintain client assets as the qualified custodian or use a related person qualified custodian rather than maintaining client assets with an independent qualified custodian may present higher risk to clients. In recognition of such risk, SEC also imposed in its 2009 rule amendments a new internal control reporting requirement on advisers that maintain client assets or use related person qualified custodians (see fig. 3 above). The internal control report must include an opinion of an independent public accountant as to whether suitable controls are in place and operating effectively to meet control objectives relating to custodial services. This includes the safeguarding of assets held by the adviser or related person. An adviser that directly maintains client assets as a qualified custodian or maintains client assets with a related person qualified custodian must obtain or receive from its related person an internal control report annually from an accountant that is registered with and subject to regular inspection by PCAOB. Advisers qualifying for a surprise examination exception because of their use of a related person but operationally independent custodian still must obtain an internal control report from their related person.

### *Related Record-Keeping Requirements*

In conjunction with the amendments to the custody rule, SEC also amended its record-keeping rule.[27] The revised rule requires advisers to maintain a copy of any internal control report obtained or received pursuant to the SEC custody rule.[28] The rule also requires advisers, if applicable, to maintain a memorandum describing the basis upon which they determined that the presumption that any related person is not operationally independent under the custody rule has been overcome.[29] According to SEC, requiring an adviser to retain a copy of these items provides SEC examiners with important information about the safeguards in place and assists SEC examiners in assessing custody-related risks.

## Compliance Requirements and Costs Vary

Around 4,400 advisers, about 45 percent of all SEC-registered advisers, reported having custody (for reasons other than their authority to deduct fees) of over \$14 trillion in client assets as of April 1, 2013.[30] In addition, around 500 advisers, about 11 percent of the 4,400 advisers with custody, reported serving as the qualified custodian or having a related person qualified custodian of client assets. As discussed, the SEC custody rule imposes certain minimum requirements generally on all advisers with custody, but not all of the rule's requirements apply to all advisers. Instead, the rule generally imposes more stringent requirements on advisers whose custodial arrangements, in SEC's view, pose greater risk of misappropriation or other misuse of client assets.

According to representatives from industry associations and advisers that we interviewed, advisers can incur an array of direct and indirect costs to comply with the SEC custody rule. Direct costs, such as accounting and legal fees paid by advisers, tend to be more easily measured than indirect costs, such as staff hours spent by an adviser to comply with the rule. The representatives told us that compliance costs include the following:

- Initial costs: After the SEC custody rule was amended in 2009, advisers initially incurred indirect costs (largely management and staff hours) and, in some cases, direct costs (largely consulting or legal fees) to interpret the amendments and comply with the rule's new or amended requirements. For example, one adviser told us that his firm hired a law firm to help it interpret the amended rule, hired a part-time person for 6 months to review and determine over which accounts the adviser had custody, and utilized staff to reprogram the firm's information system to code accounts under custody. Another adviser told us that his firm had the necessary in-house expertise to interpret the amended rule but nevertheless expended considerable internal resources for training staff about the surprise examination requirements and searching for and hiring an accountant to conduct the examinations.
- Recurring costs: On an ongoing basis, advisers incur indirect and, in some cases, direct costs to comply with the custody rule. Advisers expend internal staff hours to maintain records and prepare required statements and disclosures, including Form ADV (the form that advisers use to register with SEC and must update annually). Advisers

subject to the surprise examination or internal control report requirement expend staff hours to prepare for and facilitate such reviews. For example, an official from an adviser told us that the firm expends considerable staff hours each year educating the accountant about the firm's operations, generating reports for and providing other support to the accountant, and answering questions from clients related to the examination. In addition, these advisers may incur the direct cost of the examination or audit, and the amount of these fees varies from adviser to adviser (as discussed later in the report).

Although advisers to pooled investment vehicles often undergo an annual financial statement audit in lieu of a surprise examination, they incur the indirect and direct costs associated with the audit.

According to SEC staff and representatives from three industry associations that we spoke with, surprise examinations and internal control reporting, if applicable, tended to be two of the more costly requirements associated with SEC's custody rule. In contrast, record-keeping costs were not significant, according to officials from three associations, two securities law attorneys, and seven of the advisers with whom we spoke.

### *Cost of Surprise Examinations*

According to representatives we interviewed from four accounting firms, their surprise examination fee is based on the amount of hours required to conduct the examinations, which is a function of a number of factors. One of the most important factors is the number of client accounts under custody, which influences the number of accounts that accountants will need to review to verify custody. Other factors affecting examination cost include the amount of client assets under custody, types of securities under custody, and number and location of the custodians. Over 1,300 advisers with custody of client assets, about 30 percent of the 4,400 advisers with custody, reported being subject to the surprise examination requirement as of April 1, 2013. Importantly, these advisers vary widely in terms of the number of their clients under custody—reported by advisers as ranging from 1 client to over 1 million clients—and other factors that affect the cost of surprise examinations. Consequently, the cost of surprise examinations varies widely across the advisers.

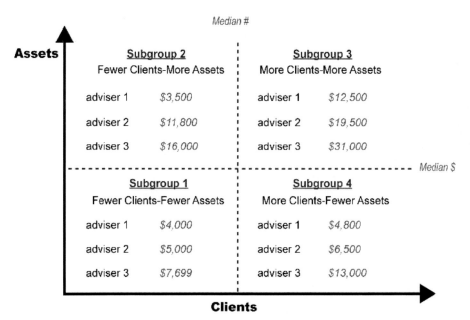

Figure 4. Surprise Examination Costs for 12 SEC-Registered Investment Advisers, 2012.

Source: GAO analysis of SEC-registered adviser and accountant interviews.

Note: Based on Form ADV data as of December 2012, approximately 1,300 advisers reported undergoing surprise examinations. We divided these advisers into four subgroups based on whether the number of their clients under custody and amount of their client assets under custody were above or below the group's median value for the two variables. Thus, at one end of the spectrum, subgroup 1 includes advisers whose number of clients and amount of client assets under custody were both below the group's median values. At the other end of the spectrum, subgroup 3 includes advisers whose number of clients and amount of client assets were both above the group's median values. Within each subgroup, we then selected advisers whose client assets were around the subgroup's median value. (For additional information see app. I.)

Although no comprehensive data exist on surprise examination costs, several industry associations and SEC have provided estimates. In response to SEC's 2009 proposed amendments to the custody rule, industry associations provided SEC with cost estimates. For example, the Investment Advisers Association, representing SEC-registered advisers, estimated that surprise examinations would likely cost each of its members between $20,000 and $300,000.

The Securities Industry and Financial Markets Association, representing major asset management firms and custodians, estimated that surprise examination costs would range from $8,000 to $275,000 for each of its members. However, these estimates were based on the then-current SEC guidance to accountants that required verification of 100 percent of client assets under custody. In conjunction with its 2009 final rule amendment, SEC issued a companion release that revised the guidance to allow accountants to verify a sample of client assets.[31] In its 2009 final amendments to the custody rule, SEC estimated the cost of surprise examinations for large, medium, and small advisers in consideration of revisions to its guidance that allowed accountants to verify a sample of client assets. In particular, SEC estimated that the average cost of a surprise examination for large, medium, and small advisers would be $125,000, $20,000, and $10,000, respectively.[32]

To help determine the range of potential costs of surprise examinations for selected subgroups of advisers, we obtained data on the examination fees for 12 advisers.[33] As shown in figure 4, the fees that the 12 advisers paid to their independent public accountants for recent surprise examinations ranged from $3,500 to $31,000. Figure 4 also shows that fees varied among advisers we selected within each of the subgroups. For example, fees in subgroup 2 ranged from $3,500 to $16,000 for the three advisers we selected.[34]

### Cost of Internal Control Reports

Fewer than 500 advisers, about 11 percent of advisers with custody, reported obtaining internal control reports as of April 1, 2013. Similar to surprise examination costs, the cost of internal control reports varies based on a number of factors, such as the size of and services offered by the qualified custodian. In its final 2009 rule, SEC estimated that an internal control report relating to custody would cost, on average, $250,000.[35] According to officials from four accounting firms we spoke with, internal control reporting costs for their clients may range from $25,000 to $500,000. Unlike with surprise examinations and associated costs, some advisers and their related person qualified custodians may obtain internal control reports for reasons other than the custody rule.

For example, representatives from two industry associations told us that institutional investors commonly require their custodians that are related persons to their advisers to obtain internal control reports.[36]

# SEC VIEWS ADVISERS USING RELATED BUT OPERATIONALLY INDEPENDENT CUSTODIANS AS POSING RELATIVELY LOW RISK

SEC provided certain investment advisers with an exception from the surprise examination requirement because their custodial practices pose relatively lower risk or they adopted other controls to protect client assets, such as annual financial statement audits. The broad range of industry, regulatory, and other parties that we interviewed generally supported or did not have a view on the surprise examination exception provided to advisers using related but operationally independent custodians to hold client assets.

## SEC Excepted Advisers from Surprise Examination Requirement for Several Reasons

Although SEC's 2009 proposed amendments to the custody rule would have required all registered advisers with custody of client assets to undergo a surprise examination, SEC provided exceptions from the requirement to certain advisers in the final 2009 rule amendments. In the 2009 amendments, SEC expressed that the surprise examination requirement should help deter fraud because advisers will know their client assets are subject to verification at any time and, thus, may be less likely to engage in misconduct.[37] SEC noted that if fraud does occur, the examination will increase the likelihood that the fraud will be detected earlier.[38]

As discussed earlier, advisers deemed to have custody solely because of their authority to deduct fees from client accounts are excluded from the surprise examination requirement. In SEC's view, the magnitude of the risks of client losses from overcharging advisory fees did not warrant the costs of obtaining a surprise examination. Also excluded from the requirement are advisers to a pooled investment vehicle that undergo annual audits of their financial statements by an independent public accountant and distribute the audited statements to investors. According to SEC, procedures performed by accountants during the course of a financial statement audit provide meaningful protections to investors, and the surprise examination would not significantly add to these protections.[39]

Additionally, SEC provided a limited exception to advisers that are (1) deemed to have custody solely because a related person serves as the custodian and holds client assets and (2) operationally independent of the custodian. According to SEC, client assets may be at greater risk when maintained by an adviser's related person. However, SEC noted that firms under common ownership but operationally independent of each other present substantially lower client custodial risks than those that are not.[40] According to SEC, the risk is lower because the misuse of client assets would tend to require collusion between the adviser and custodian employees, which is not significantly different than would be necessary to engage in similar misconduct between unaffiliated organizations.[41] Under the custody rule, a related person is presumed not to be operationally independent unless each of the following conditions is met and no other circumstances can reasonably be expected to compromise the operational independence of the related person:

- client assets in the custody of the related person are not subject to claims of the adviser's creditors;
- advisory personnel do not have custody or possession of, or direct or indirect access to, client assets of which the related person has custody, or the power to control the disposition of such client assets to third parties for the benefit of the adviser or its related persons, or otherwise have the opportunity to misappropriate such client assets;
- advisory personnel and personnel of the related person who have access to advisory client assets are not under common supervision; and
- advisory personnel do not hold any position with the related person or share premises with the related person.[42]

Although an adviser that meets these conditions would not be required to undergo a surprise examination, the adviser still would be required to comply with the rule's other applicable provisions, including obtaining an internal control report from its related person. SEC emphasized that an adviser that has custody due to reasons in addition to a related person having custody cannot rely on the exception because it is only applicable if an adviser has custody solely because its related person has custody. For example, an adviser that has custody because he or she serves as a trustee with respect to client assets held in an account at a broker-dealer that is a related person could not rely on the exception from the surprise examination on the grounds that the broker-dealer was operationally independent, because the adviser has custody for reasons other than through its operationally independent related person.

## A Limited Number of Advisers Do Not Undergo Surprise Examinations Because They Use Related but Operationally Independent Custodians

As of April 1, 2013, 169 registered advisers reported having custody of client assets and using related but operationally independent custodians and not undergoing an annual surprise examination for certain clients.[43]

These advisers account for around 2 percent of all SEC-registered advisers and about 42 percent of the approximately 400 SEC-registered advisers that have a related person holding client assets. These advisers collectively have over $6 trillion in regulatory assets under management and custody of over $1 trillion of client assets. The structure of large institutions with functionally independent subsidiaries tends to lend itself to meet the operationally independent conditions. More specifically, we identified some advisers using related but operationally independent custodians that are part of large financial institutions with numerous subsidiaries, such as Deutsche Bank, JPMorgan Chase, Morgan Stanley, and Wells Fargo. According to SEC staff, this outcome is to be expected given that the adviser and custodian staff cannot be considered operationally independent while under common supervision and sharing the same premises.

If advisers currently qualifying for an exception from the surprise examination requirement were required to undergo such examinations, the costs of the examinations would likely vary considerably across the advisers. Like advisers currently subject to the surprise examination requirement, advisers excepted from the requirement vary considerably in terms of the factors that affect the cost of the examinations. For example, the number of clients these advisers had under custody ranged from 1 client to over 500,000 clients, as of April 1, 2013. Similarly, the amount of client assets under their custody ranged from $680,000 to $320 billion.

## Views on the Surprise Examination's Exception and Effectiveness

The broad range of industry, accounting firms, and other parties we interviewed largely told us that they either support or do not have a view on the surprise examination exception. However, several of these representatives said that the exception's operationally independent conditions were too stringent or difficult to meet.[44] None of the investment advisers we interviewed use a related custodian to hold client assets, and most did not have a view on the exception or SEC's rationale. The North American Securities Administrators Association (NASAA) staff told us that when a custodian is a related person of the adviser, ensuring that the adviser meets and complies with the operationally independent conditions would require the firm to conduct a thorough analysis of its operations and any changes that may affect the custodian's operational independence. The staff further noted that NASAA's custody model rule for use by state securities regulators, unlike the SEC custody rule, does not include an exception from the surprise examination requirement based on the concept of operational independence between an investment adviser and a custodian that is a related person.[45] An investor advocacy representative told us that he generally opposes allowing advisers to use related custodians, but if that were allowed, he said that, in his opinion, the surprise examination exception would be appropriate for only large, complex entities subject to existing regulation, such as banks and broker-dealers.

Many of the industry, regulatory, and other parties we interviewed agreed with SEC's view that surprise examinations can help to deter fraud. However, some told us that one of the examination's weaknesses is that accountants must rely on advisers to provide them with a complete list of the client assets under custody to verify. According to some of these representatives, an adviser defrauding a client could omit that client's account from the list provided to the accountant to avoid detection. Officials from an accounting firm told us that no infallible procedure exists to test the completeness of the client list, given that the list must come from the adviser. According to SEC staff, an adviser with custody and intent on defrauding its clients also may not register with SEC or, if it does, may not report that it has custody of client assets or hire an accountant to conduct a surprise examination. SEC staff also noted that the surprise examination requirement, like any regulation, cannot prevent fraud 100 percent of the time but that it helps deter such misconduct.

SEC data indicate that surprise examinations have identified compliance issues and helped target higher-risk advisers for examination. SEC staff told us that since the 2009 custody rule amendments became effective in March 2010, auditors conducting surprise examinations have found around 100 advisers with one or more instances of material noncompliance with the rule, such as failing to maintain client securities at a qualified custodian. According to SEC staff, the results of surprise examinations serve as an early warning of potential risks and are used by staff to help assess the risk level of advisers and, in turn, select advisers for SEC examination. For example, in March 2013, SEC's Office of Compliance Inspections and Examinations issued a

"Risk Alert" that noted that about 33 percent (over 140 examinations) of recent SEC examinations found custody-related deficiencies.[46] These deficiencies included failures to comply with the rule's surprise examination requirement and qualified custodian requirements and resulted in actions ranging from immediate remediation to enforcement referrals and subsequent litigation.

## AGENCY COMMENTS

We requested comments from SEC, but none were provided. SEC provided technical comments, which we incorporated, as appropriate.

A. Nicole Clowers
Director
Financial Markets and Community Investment Issues

## APPENDIX I: OBJECTIVES, SCOPE, AND METHODOLOGY

This report describes (1) the requirements of and costs associated with the Securities and Exchange Commission (SEC) custody rule, including any related record-keeping requirements, for registered investment advisers, and (2) SEC's rationale for not requiring advisers using related but operationally independent custodians to undergo surprise examinations, and the number and characteristics of such advisers.

To address both objectives, we analyzed SEC's record-keeping and custody rules under the Investment Advisers Act of 1940 to document compliance requirements (e.g., surprise examinations and internal control reports) for SEC-registered investment advisers. Furthermore, we reviewed proposed and final SEC amendments to the custody rule, comment letters, and other information, such as GAO and other studies, to analyze how and why the custody rule requirements have changed, particularly the surprise examination requirement and exceptions, and obtain information on compliance costs. We analyzed publicly available data in the Investment Adviser Registration Depository (IARD) to identify the number of SEC-registered investment advisers and information advisers reported about their compliance with the SEC custody rule's requirements. IARD data are submitted by advisers in

Form ADV, which is used by advisers to register with SEC and must be updated annually by advisers.[1] We assessed the reliability of Form ADV data by interviewing SEC staff and testing the data for errors, and we determined the data were sufficiently reliable for our purposes. Specifically, we interviewed SEC staff about the IARD database and Form ADV to understand how the data are collected, what types of edit checks are incorporated into the system, and the staff's overall views of the system's data reliability with respect to our purposes. We also performed electronic testing to identify potential errors, and we discussed analysis methodology considerations, such as excluding particular records, with SEC staff for any inconsistencies that we identified. For the purposes of our final analysis, we excluded records for advisers that reported zero as the regulatory assets under management or total clients and any record with the latest Form ADV filing date older than January 2012.

To obtain data on the costs of complying with the SEC custody rule, particularly its surprise examination and internal control report requirements, and other information, we interviewed a limited number of investment advisers and accounting firms. Based on Form ADV data as of December 3, 2012, we identified approximately 1,300 advisers that reported undergoing surprise examinations.

To systematically target advisers and firms, we first divided the total group of advisers that reported undergoing surprise examinations into four subgroups based on whether the amount of their client assets under custody were above or below the group's median value of approximately $101 million and whether their number of clients under custody were above or below the median of 19 clients, as shown in figure 5.

Thus, at one end of the spectrum, subgroup 1 includes advisers whose number of clients and amount of client assets under custody were both below the group's median values. At the other end of the spectrum, subgroup 3 includes advisers whose number of clients and amount of client assets were both above the group's median values. Within each subgroup, we then selected advisers whose client assets were around the subgroup's median value. For the 12 selected advisers, we interviewed eight of the advisers and interviewed four accountants who conducted the surprise examinations for the other four advisers.

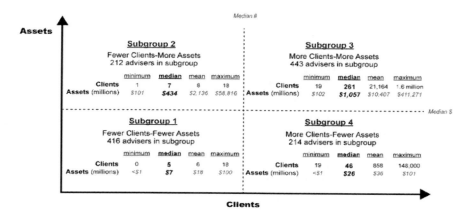

Source: GAO analysis of Form ADV data as of December 3, 2012.

Figure 5. SEC-Registered Advisers That Underwent Surprise Examinations by Number of Client Accounts and Client Assets under Custody, as of December 3, 2012.

To obtain information on the cost of complying with the custody rule and other information, we also interviewed regulators, including SEC staff, officials from the North American Securities Administrators Association, and a representative from a state securities authority, and representatives from investment adviser, accountant, investor advocacy, and other associations, including the American Institute of Certified Public Accountants, American Bankers Association, Financial Services Institute, Fund Democracy, Investment Advisers Association, Managed Futures Association, Private Equity Growth and Capital Council, and Securities Industry and Financial Markets Association. In addition, we interviewed two securities law attorneys.

We conducted this performance audit from September 2012 through July 2013 in accordance with generally accepted government auditing standards. Those standards require that we plan and perform the audit to obtain sufficient, appropriate evidence to provide a reasonable basis for our findings and conclusions based on our audit objectives. We believe that the evidence obtained provides a reasonable basis for our findings and conclusions based on our audit objectives.

## End Notes

[1] 17 C.F.R. § 275.206(4)-2(d)(2).
[2] *See* 75 Fed. Reg. 1456, 1457, 1475 (2010).

[3] 15 U.S.C. § 80b-6(4) (added by Pub. L. No. 86-750, sec. 9, 74 Stat. 885, 887 (1960)); Adoption of Rule 206(4)-2, Investment Advisers Act Release No. 123, 1962 SEC LEXIS 655 (Feb. 27, 1962).

[4] Custody of Funds or Securities of Clients by Investment Advisers, Investment Advisers Act Release No. 2176, 68 Fed. Reg. 56,692 (Oct. 1, 2003). Under the amended rule, advisers with custody of client assets were required to maintain the assets with qualified custodians. If the qualified custodian sent account statements directly to the adviser's clients at least quarterly, the adviser was relieved from having to send its own account statements and undergo an annual surprise examination.

[5] Custody of Funds or Securities of Clients by Investment Advisers, Investment Advisers Act Release No. 2968 (Dec. 30, 2009), 75 Fed. Reg. 1456 (Jan. 11, 2010).

[6] In the rule, SEC has set out a number of conditions that an adviser must meet to satisfy the definition of "operationally independent." We discuss those conditions in detail later in this report.

[7] Pub. L. No. 111-203, § 412, 124 Stat.1376, 1577 (2010).

[8] Form ADV is the form used by investment advisers to register with both SEC and state securities authorities. Form ADV consists of two parts. Part 1 collects information about the adviser's business, ownership, clients, employees, business practices (especially those involving potential conflicts with clients), and any disciplinary events of the adviser or its employees. Part 2 collects information from client brochures and brochure supplements.

[9] For additional information about investment advisers, see SEC, *Study on Investment Advisers and Broker-Dealers, as Required by Section 913 of the Dodd-Frank Wall Street Reform and Consumer Protection Act* (Washington, D.C.: January 2011).

[10] 15 U.S.C. § 80b-2(a)(11).

[11] *See* 15 U.S.C. §§ 80b-3, 80b-3a. For a more detailed discussion, see SEC, Investment Adviser Regulation Office, Division of Investment Management, *Regulation of Investment Advisers* (March 2013).

[12] 15 U.S.C. § 80b-3a. Unless an exemption is available, all advisers with their principal office and place of business in Wyoming and mid-sized advisers with their principal office and place of business in New York are not "subject to examination" and must register with SEC. In terms of regulatory assets under management, small-sized advisers generally have less than $25 million, mid-sized generally more than $25 million but less than $100 million, and large-sized generally more than $100 million. Regulatory assets under management are the sum of assets under management or securities portfolios for which the adviser provides continuous and regular supervisory or management services and include, for accounts of private funds, the amount of any uncalled capital commitments as of the date of filing. Advisers are instructed to determine the amount based on the current market value of the assets as determined within 90 days prior to the date of filing.

[13] The statistics are based on Form ADV data. We excluded from our statistics advisers that had not filed updated Form ADV information since December 1, 2011, and advisers that reported no, or zero, regulatory assets under management or advisory clients.

[14] 17 C.F.R. § 275.206(4)-2(d)(2).

[15] *Id.* A related person includes anyone who controls, is controlled by, or is under common control with the adviser. 17 C.F.R. § 275.206(4)-2(d)(7).

[16] 17 C.F.R. § 275.206(4)-2(d)(6). Entities that can serve as custodians include: brokers, which are in the business of effecting transactions in securities for the account of others; dealers, which are in the business of buying and selling securities for their own account through a broker or otherwise; and futures commission merchants which solicit or accept orders for

the purchase or sale of any commodity for future delivery on or subject to the rules of any exchange and that accept payment from or extend credit to those whose orders are accepted.

[17] For example, banks are regulated by the prudential regulators; registered broker-dealers are regulated by SEC and the Financial Industry Regulatory Authority; and registered futures commission merchants are regulated by the Commodity Futures Trading Commission and National Futures Association.

[18] 17 C.F.R. § 275.206(4)-2(a)(3).

[19] 17 C.F.R. § 275.206(4)-2(a)(4).

[20] Adoption of Rule 206(4)-2, Investment Advisers Act Release No. 123, 1962 SEC LEXIS 655 (Feb. 27, 1962).

[21] 68 Fed. Reg. 56,692 (Oct. 1, 2003).

[22] 67 Fed. Reg. 48,579, 48,583 (July 25, 2002).

[23] 74 Fed. Reg. 25,354, 25,355 (May 27, 2009).

[24] *Id.* at 25,356.

[25] According to SEC, an adviser that has custody for reasons that are separate from having an operationally independent related person with custody may be subject to the surprise examination requirement.

[26] PCAOB is a nonprofit corporation established by Congress to oversee the audits of public companies in order to protect the interests of investors and further the public interest in the preparation of informative, accurate, and independent audit reports. PCAOB also oversees the audits of broker-dealers, including compliance reports filed pursuant to federal securities laws, to promote investor protection. In addition, the SEC custody rule requires advisers to pooled investment vehicles that comply with the rule by distributing audited financial statements to investors to also obtain an audit upon liquidation of the pool when the liquidation occurs before the fund's fiscal year-end.

[27] 75 Fed. Reg. 1483 (Jan. 11, 2010) (amending 17 C.F.R. § 275.204-2).

[28] 17 C.F.R. § 275.204-2(a)(17)(iii).

[29] 17 C.F.R. § 275.204-2(b)(5).

[30] The total reflects advisers that reported they or their related person had custody of client assets. Form ADV does not include a field to track advisers deemed to have custody of client assets solely because of their ability to deduct management fees from client accounts. The total client assets under custody may be overestimated due to advisers that may have erroneously reported duplicate account assets for themselves and a related person.

[31] Commission Guidance Regarding Independent Public Accountant Engagements Performed Pursuant to Rule 206(4)-2, Investment Advisers Act Release No. 2969, 97 SEC Docket 1896 (Dec. 30, 2009). According to SEC, the commenters based their cost estimates for surprise examinations on the previous guidance for accountants, which required verification of 100 percent of client assets. SEC expects that the estimates would be significantly lower if they reflected the current procedures for the surprise examination, which allows for the use of sampling of client accounts. The current procedures were described in the guidance for accountants issued in a companion release and became effective March 12, 2010.

[32] 75 Fed. Reg. at 1473. SEC defined large firms as those advisers subject to a surprise examination that either served as a qualified custodian or had a related person serve as a qualified custodian. The remaining firms subject to the surprise examinations were defined as small or medium based on the number of their clients relative to the average number of clients for the entire group.

[33] For additional information, see appendix I.

[34] Our cost data may not be indicative of the examination costs of other advisers in the same subgroup because factors other than the number of clients and assets under custody can affect costs. In addition, because we selected advisers near each subgroup's median value, we did not obtain cost data from the largest advisers, whose examination costs may be closer in line with SEC's $125,000 cost estimate for large advisers.

[35] 75 Fed. Reg. at 1482.

[36] Similarly, in its 2009 proposed amendments to the custody rule, SEC stated that it understood that mutual fund custodians obtain internal control reports for other reasons. 74 Fed. Reg. at 25,370 n.165.

[37] 75 Fed. Reg. at 1475.

[38] *Id.*

[39] The financial statement audit must be prepared in accordance with generally accepted accounting principles and the audit must be done in accordance with generally accepted auditing standards. In a financial statement audit, the accountant performs procedures comparable to those that would be performed in a surprise examination, including verifying the existence of funds and securities and obtaining confirmation from investors.

[40] 75 Fed. Reg. at 1464.

[41] *Id.*

[42] 17 C.F.R. § 275.206(4)-2(d)(5).

[43] Of the 169 registered investment advisers, 41 of them qualified for an exception from the surprise examination requirement for some of their clients under custody but underwent a surprise examination for other clients under custody. For example, an adviser might have custody of certain client assets because it solely held such assets with a related but operationally independent client but may have custody of other client assets because it served as a trustee for those accounts.

[44] The officials said the requirements that both adviser and custodian staff cannot (1) be under common supervision and (2) share the same premises were examples of conditions that were difficult to meet. More specifically, one official told us that a number of large banks have related advisers and custodians that share a building but are located on different floors and thus would have to move staff to another building to qualify for the exception.

[45] NASAA Model Custody Rule under the Uniform Securities Act of 1956 (amended Apr. 15, 2013). NASAA Model Custody Rule under the Uniform Securities Act of 2002 (amended Apr. 15, 2013).

[46] SEC's Office of Compliance Inspections and Examinations, National Exam Program Risk Alert, *Significant Deficiencies Involving Adviser Custody and Safety of Client Assets*, vol. 3, issue 1 (Mar. 4, 2013).

# End Notes for Appendix I

[1] Form ADV consists of two parts. Part 1 collects information about the adviser's business, ownership, clients, employees, business practices (especially those involving potential conflicts with clients), and any disciplinary events of the adviser or its employees. Part 2 collects information required in client brochures and brochure supplements.

# INDEX

## C

**D**

## H

## G

## I

**Y**